## Praise for *A Course in*

'*Excellent, excellent, wonderful, wonderfu.., ...,p.y meaningful, just what the doctor ordered! Simple, easy to read and filled with neat little stories, this book will go far in helping students of* A Course in Miracles *understand some of its most basic concepts and principles.*'

— **Jon Mundy PhD,** author of *Living* A Course in Miracles

'*A Course in Miracles Made Easy is an impressive and welcomed marvel. It's a gem! There are wonderful stories here, along with in-depth and deeply personal sharing. In this terrific book, Alan Cohen truly knows how to teach. Heads-up, ACIM students and teachers: a new voice from an accomplished author has entered the ACIM author troupe, and I for one am very grateful.*'

— **Rev. Tony Ponticello,** Executive Minister, Community Miracles Center

'*Alan Cohen describes* A Course in Miracles *as a map out of hell – a way out of the ego mind-set of fear, unworthiness, lack and separation. In this brilliant commentary, Alan shows us how to read the map!*'

— **Robert Holden PhD,** author of *Holy Shift!: 365 Daily Meditations from* A Course in Miracles

'*Alan Cohen is a respected author who has taught these principles for years. Recently,* A Course in Miracles *has risen to the very forefront of his life and work. In this book, he now brings his clarity, spiritual insight and joy to teaching the Course. Thank you, Alan, for this beautiful, practical and timely book, which is sure to be a boon to dedicated students and newcomers alike.*'

— **Ian Patrick,** founder and manager of the Miracle Network in the U.K.

'*A Course in Miracles Made Easy is a beautifully helpful gift for any 'seeker' to appreciate and savour. Alan's use of wit and wisdom to illustrate the ACIM message is a real treat. Thanks, Alan!*'

— **Tom Carpenter,** author of *Dialogue on Awakening*

'*For many, the impenetrability of* A Course in Miracles *is such that it might as well be written in a foreign language. Fortunately, books like this one exist. Coming from insight, heart and joy,* **A Course in Miracles Made Easy** *is one of the best primers to ACIM I've ever read. Highly recommended.*'

— **Kenneth Bok,** ACIM YouTube show host

# A
# COURSE
# IN
# MIRACLES

*made easy*

# ALSO BY ALAN COHEN

*Are You as Happy as Your Dog?*
*Dare to Be Yourself*
*A Deep Breath of Life\**
*A Daily Dose of Sanity\**
*Don't Get Lucky, Get Smart*
*The Dragon Doesn't Live Here Anymore*
*Radical Contentment\**
*The Grace Factor*
*Handle with Prayer\**
*Happily Even After\**
*Have You Hugged a Monster Today?*
*I Had It All the Time*
*Joy Is My Compass*
*Lifestyles of the Rich in Spirit*
*Linden's Last Life*
*Looking In for Number One*
*Mr. Everit's Secret*
*My Father's Voice*
*The Peace That You Seek*
*Relax into Wealth*
*Rising in Love*
*Setting the Seen*
*Why Your Life Sucks and What You Can Do about It*
*Wisdom of the Heart*

\*Available from Hay House

Please visit:

Hay House UK: www.hayhouse.co.uk
Hay House USA: www.hayhouse.com®
Hay House Australia: www.hayhouse.com.au
Hay House India: www.hayhouse.co.in

# A COURSE IN MIRACLES

*made easy*

## Mastering the Journey from Fear to Love

ALAN COHEN

**HAY HOUSE**

Carlsbad, California • New York City
London • Sydney • New Delhi

**Published in the United Kingdom by:**
Hay House UK Ltd, The Sixth Floor, Watson House,
54 Baker Street, London W1U 7BU
Tel: +44 (0)20 3927 7290; Fax: +44 (0)20 3927 7291; www.hayhouse.co.uk

**Published in the United States of America by:**
Hay House Inc., PO Box 5100, Carlsbad, CA 92018-5100
Tel: (1) 760 431 7695 or (800) 654 5126
Fax: (1) 760 431 6948 or (800) 650 5115; www.hayhouse.com

**Published in Australia by:**
Hay House Australia Ltd, 18/36 Ralph St, Alexandria NSW 2015
Tel: (61) 2 9669 4299; Fax: (61) 2 9669 4144; www.hayhouse.com.au

**Published in India by:**
Hay House Publishers India, Muskaan Complex, Plot No.3, B-2,
Vasant Kunj, New Delhi 110 070
Tel: (91) 11 4176 1620; Fax: (91) 11 4176 1630; www.hayhouse.co.in

Text © Alan Cohen, 2015

The moral rights of the author have been asserted.

The information given in this book should not be treated as a substitute for professional medical advice; always consult a medical practitioner. Any use of information in this book is at the reader's discretion and risk. Neither the author nor the publisher can be held responsible for any loss, claim or damage arising out of the use, or misuse, of the suggestions made, the failure to take medical advice or for any material on third party websites.

A catalogue record for this book is available from the British Library.

ISBN: 978-1-78180-631-9

Cover design: Julie Davison • Interior design: Nick C. Welch

All quotes from A Course in Miracles© are from the Third Edition, published in 2007 by the Foundation for Inner Peace, P.O. Box 598, Mill Valley, CA 94942-0598. www.acim.org and info@acim.org

Printed and bound by CPI Group (UK) Ltd, Croydon CR0 4YY

*To Cliff and Alden,*
*who lived it*

# CONTENTS

# PREFACE

"'Do you want to know how long it takes a person to tear up *A Course in Miracles* and throw it into the ocean?'" a fellow wrote to Saul Steinberg of Coleman Graphics, the initial printer of *A Course in Miracles* (ACIM). Saul was showing me around the Coleman warehouse, stacked to the ceiling with piles of small cardboard boxes, each containing three thick blue hardcover books that comprised the original form of ACIM. "Six months later the same guy sent me another letter asking me to please send him another copy of the Course."

We both laughed. The story was familiar. Everyone who does the Course experiences confusion and resistance. How many times have I heard, "I got the book a while ago, read bits and pieces, but I couldn't understand it. I started doing the Workbook Lessons, but stopped. I know the Course is powerful and could change my life, but I have a hard time applying it. I hope to get back to it someday." One student told me, "I opened the book for the first time after I purchased it, and the receipt fell out—dated ten years earlier!" Author and teacher Robert Holden quipped that "*A Course in Miracles* is the only book that has been purchased by millions but read by only a few."

Why would a teaching so magnificent, with such capacity to heal and transform lives in the most important ways, seem so hard? Why does truth so simple appear to be abstruse, cryptic, and mystifying? *A Course in Miracles,* ego argues, *is too hard to understand. Too long and complicated. Too Christian. Not Christian enough. Too psychological—reminds me of therapy. Why doesn't it ever say "she"? I don't have time. I have too much to do at work. The print is too small. The pages are too thin—reminds me of the Bible. I already took a Tony Robbins seminar. The dog ate the Workbook. I'm too stressed to focus. I'll read it when the kids go off to college. Some of the*

*Course's statements are downright insulting. I'll wait for the movie to
come out. How do I know that the psychologist who wrote it didn't make
it all up? I just wish it were easier.*

Ironically, *A Course in Miracles* is *already* easy. One might say
it's the easiest thing in the world, because it springs from a source
far beyond the convolutions the world prescribes. Love, healing,
and genuine forgiveness are ultimately far easier than self-doubt,
worry, wrestling with relationships, fighting over money, and la-
boring to figure out how to fix all that is broken. Letting go is far
easier than doggedly clinging, trust more empowering than resistance. *A Course in Miracles* is the ultimate answer to the question
*How easy could my life be?*

Your journey through life was never meant to be a struggle.
Everything difficult is the nightmare of fear superimposed over
the presence of love. A poetic passage from Chapter 14, Section
VI, of the Text describes how easy our walk can be when we let it:

> When you have learned how to decide with God, all
> decisions become as easy and as right as breathing. There
> is no effort, and you will be led as gently as if you were
> being carried down a quiet path in summer.

The purpose of the book you are holding is to help set your
foot on that easier path. We are going to bring *A Course in Miracles* down to earth; translate its lofty, far-reaching principles into
practical, easy-to-understand tools; and enable you to apply its
truth so your life gets only better. I want to extricate you from any
confusion about ACIM, dissolve its apparent density, demystify its
lofty truths, and show you how utterly simple it really is. *A Course
in Miracles* is, quite simply, a map out of hell. Workbook Lesson 97
tells us that if you apply the Lesson well, you can save a thousand
years or more of struggling. If this book can save you even a portion of that time, our time together will be well spent.

You can benefit from this book if you are an ACIM student
who wishes to deepen your understanding of the Course, or if
you have never studied or practiced the Course, or you never will.
While I encourage you to explore the Course, even if you do not,

you can grasp its essence here. If you gain even an inkling of what ACIM has to offer, you are blessed.

The adventure we are about to take together could be the most important one of your life. Let's unravel what brings you pain and gain relief from the insane entanglements the world engenders. Let's dissolve the illusions that have kept you small and reveal the truth that makes you magnificent. Let's remember what makes life worth living and let all else go back to the nothingness from which it came.

## My Journey with the Course

On a cold winter evening I sat at my desk staring at the small, brown cardboard box that had just arrived in the mail. I tried to imagine its contents, but couldn't. I simply knew that what was in the box was important. Yet I had no idea how crucial the contents would prove to be in my life and the lives of millions.

I had been hearing about *A Course in Miracles* for a year, seeing posters on bulletin boards and overhearing snippets of conversations. I was skeptical. After treading the personal-growth path for a long time, I had seen too much hype and charlatanry. The title turned me off. *A Course in Miracles.* Was it another New Age come-on, dangling powers of wizardry before naïve seekers? Or a cult enticing lost souls to feed the coffers of a distant guru? I wanted nothing to do with low-level magic. Another metaphysical sideshow held no allure for me.

Then an article in *Psychology Today* caught my eye. A hokey illustration depicted three golden books descending from the heavens to a man walking along a street. In spite of the cheesy graphic, I read the article. To my surprise, I was intrigued. The Course was not what I had assumed it to be. It seemed more spiritual than material, more about consciousness than stuff. By the end of my reading, I felt drawn to get a copy of the Course—more of a gut knowing than an intellectual decision. I now recognize that inner voice to be what the Course calls the Holy Spirit. But at the time

I had no name for such guidance. All I knew was that I wanted to know what was between the covers of those books.

Then there was the price: $40 plus shipping. In 1980, 40 bucks was a lot for me. I was renting a room in a friend's attic, practicing yoga, playing my guitar, and listening to inspirational tapes. A few part-time jobs helped me pay my $150 monthly rent. I was content. Did I really need three books for $40? Now I laugh at my hesitation. Those 40 bucks proved to be the best investment of my life.

I opened the brown box and removed the first volume, "Text" imprinted in gold leaf on the textured, navy blue hardcover. I read the introduction:

> Nothing real can be threatened.
> Nothing unreal exists.
> Herein lies the peace of God.

As I read, a power reached out from the page and engulfed me as if I had opened a portal to another dimension. I didn't understand the passage, but the energy that streamed from the book was nearly overwhelming, stimulating within me a soul excitement I had never before experienced. I closed the book, trying to absorb those words. This was going to be some ride . . .

Over the many years since that time, *A Course in Miracles* has become only more dear, meaningful, and practical in my life. Its truth becomes more alive to me every day. I can't say that I have been the best student of the Course. My resistance has too often had its way, I have given in to fear more than I care to admit, and I have been slow to put the Lessons into action. Yet when I do, I experience deep soul solace, and miracles literally occur in my world. There is no end to the Course's depth and scope. Every day I feel as if the current passage or Lesson was written just for me. The Course is real. It works. It is a gift from God.

During most of the 35 years I have been practicing the Course, I have not taught or written about it directly, but have chosen rather to weave Course principles into the fabric of my writing and teaching. During the past few years, however, I have experienced an increased appreciation and excitement for the rock-solid value of the Course. Many personal and spiritual growth methods fade and tatter over time. For me, the Course has become only more alive and powerful. No matter what other paths I have trod and what other teachers have captured my attention, I keep coming back to *A Course in Miracles*. For me, its philosophy and intention overarch all the other methods I have learned.

Now I so deeply wish to master the Course that it has risen to the forefront of my life and my work. The Course tells us that by teaching what we wish to learn, we learn it. While I hope and trust that this book will serve you well, I am writing to edify and expand my own understanding of *A Course in Miracles*.

As we move through the pages that follow, I will share with you many true stories of the ways that ACIM has profoundly affected my life and the lives of others. While some Course students complain that it is too out-of-this-world, my experience is that it reaches into the core of life on Earth, sometimes into the darkest places of mortal suffering, and transforms us right where we stand, even amidst our abysmal human frailty. Whether you find yourself in severe pain or your life is working well and you wish to make it even better, I hope that you will be inspired in the pages that follow to move to your next level of healing and awakening.

The facts of my story may be unique, but not the theme. We have all been lost, and we are all finding our way home. It is no accident that *A Course in Miracles* has come into your awareness at this time. Whether you are to study the Course intensively, or you glean even one helpful concept from this book, or you simply hear the title *A Course in Miracles* and you begin to consider the possibility that miracles exist and you can have one or many, there is a reason you and the Course have met.

Now let's discover what that is . . .

# HOW TO MAKE THE BEST USE OF THIS BOOK

When quoting from *A Course in Miracles,* I refer to the edition known as "The Only Complete Edition," published by the Foundation for Inner Peace. This edition includes a text numbering system that allows students to locate passages. For shorthand reference in this book, "T" refers to the *Text,* "W" to the *Workbook for Students,* "M" to *Manual for Teachers,* and "C" to *Clarification of Terms.* The numbers that follow each quotation refer to the section, paragraph, and sentence from which the quotation is drawn.

Here is an example of how to use the reference system:

T-2.VI.9:4–7
Text, chapter 2, section 6, paragraph 9, sentences 4 through 7
W-132.1:4
Workbook Lesson 132, paragraph 1, sentence 4
M-5.II.2.5–13
Manual for Teachers, chapter 5, section 2, paragraph 2, sentences 5 through 13
(C-Ep.1:2)
Clarification of Terms (part of Manual for Teachers), epilogue, paragraph 1, sentence 2

As you've seen already, I refer to the Course in several ways: *A Course in Miracles;* its acronym, ACIM; or simply "the Course."

This book is composed of two parts. The main body illuminates the Course's principles and how to use them to find inner peace and healing. The second part is a series of answers to frequently asked questions about specific elements and applications of the course. Rather than presenting the two sections sequentially, I have sandwiched the elements of the second section throughout the book, so you will find one question and answer after every few chapters of the main body of the work.

The chapters are ordered explaining first the most basic elements of the Course, followed by more advanced concepts and subtleties that readers who wish to really master the teachings will want to explore. You can read this book before you study the Course or simultaneously with it. Or if you never study it. One of the most important teachings of ACIM is to follow your inner guidance, so if you allow your study to be overseen by your intuition, you are putting the Course into action by the way you learn it.

Regarding the apparently religious or Christian language of ACIM, I want to explain up front that the Course is entirely non-denominational. It does not belong to the Christian religion or any other religion. Its message is universal, available to individuals who participate in any religion or no religion. Sadly, many people have had painful experiences with religion, which turns them off to any reference that reminds them of religion. ACIM does not intend to evoke that pain, but release you from it.

If, likewise, the word *God* contains a negative charge for you, feel free to substitute any term with which you feel more comfortable. *Higher Power, Source Energy, Universal Mind, Life Force, All That Is,* or any other term will work. Dr. Helen Schucman, who scribed the Course, considered herself an atheist. So if Higher Power was willing to find and uplift Helen right where she was, it can certainly find each of us right where we stand. Don't get hung up on the terminology. Instead, I invite you to pierce to the heart of the teachings.

Okay, let's get going . . .

# What Is *A Course in Miracles?*

*A Course in Miracles* is a self-study system of spiritual awakening that teaches the way to inner peace and healing through the power of love and forgiveness. The Course is composed of three volumes: *Text, Workbook for Students,* and *Manual for Teachers,* contained in one book. ACIM is available in paper and electronic format through major booksellers, online, and through teaching centers.

The Text sets forth universal truths that lead us to a life of meaning, healing, and well-being. Themes include the importance of choosing love over fear, our eternal nature as expressions of the divine, our benevolent relationship to God, our immutable innocence, the power of the mind, distinguishing between truth and illusion, transforming "special" relationships to "holy" relationships, and withdrawing the authority we have attributed to external sources. The Text explains why we hurt and how to heal.

The Text is written largely in iambic pentameter, the classic poetic form in which Shakespeare and other master poets have expressed lofty ideas. In some ways the Course is a volume of visionary poetry more than an academic treatise.

The Workbook for Students sets forth 365 days of exercises that assist the student to apply the principles to create practical and lasting life improvement. The Lessons begin very simply with just a few minutes' practice each day, and eventually increase to generate a global makeover of one's thought system and life. The Course is uncompromising in its intention to deliver liberation.

The Manual for Teachers delves into more detail regarding the application of the Course, answering more specific questions, such as "Is reincarnation true?"; "How is healing accomplished?"; and "How will the world end?" ACIM considers all students to be teachers of God, so the Manual for Teachers is for everyone.

You can study the three sections of ACIM in any order. Since the Workbook is the key to mastering the Course in daily life, I recommend that you go through the Workbook Lessons at the outset of your journey, and visit the other volumes as you feel guided. Simultaneous study will enhance your understanding.

Two related smaller pamphlets serve as addendums to the Course: *Psychotherapy: Purpose, Process and Practice* and *The Song of Prayer: Prayer, Forgiveness, Healing.*

*A Course in Miracles* is one of the most profound spiritual teachings ever to come to humanity. In its gentle yet dynamic way, the Course has touched the lives of millions of people, relieved souls from the tyranny of fear, transformed circumstances that would take a miracle to heal, and brought peace of mind to the weary. Perhaps you are among those who have already benefited from the Course—or are about to.

# 1

# THE ONLY CHOICE THAT MATTERS

While my friend and avid ACIM student Cliff Klein was watching television in the living room of his Brooklyn apartment, he heard a strange noise in the bedroom. He rose to investigate and found a burglar creeping in from the fire escape. When the intruder saw Cliff, he turned and began to flee. "Wait!" Cliff called to him. "You don't have to run. I'll help you if I can."

Stunned, the burglar stopped and slowly stepped back into the room. Cliff asked him what was going on in his life that had made him turn to stealing. The fellow told him that he had been fired from his job and lost his girlfriend. He felt powerless and angry and didn't know how he was going to pay his rent. Cliff invited the fellow to sit down and offered him a cup of coffee. Then he gave the young man some words of encouragement and handed him some cash, saying, "Come back if you want to talk some more." The fellow thanked Cliff and departed through the front door.

You have just read the cheat-sheet summary of the entire *Course in Miracles*. Every moment, the Course tells us, offers us a choice between fear and love. When Cliff Klein encountered that robber, the scenario could have taken a hundred different directions, mostly dark. But when Cliff chose to view that situation as a call for love rather than an attack, he created an entirely different outcome than he would have generated if he had acted from fear. Miracles are the natural outcome of choosing love.

Life seems overwhelming when we face an endless stream of perplexing choices: How will I connect with my life partner? Should I stay married or leave? How am I going to pay this month's bills? Is there a job that will bring me passion *and* income? How do I deal with my annoying relatives? Where on earth is my home? How will I get or stay healthy? And on and on and on. Yet behind all of these *apparent* choices, the only *real* choice is between fear and love. Fear hurts and love heals. All else is detail.

The fearful mind spins a web of complexity that makes the hardships of the world seem inescapable. ACIM tells us that life does not have to be hard and the world that fear has fabricated is entirely escapable. Boil every choice down to what heals versus what hurts, answer fear with love, and you will find the peace you seek.

> There are two teachers only, who point in different ways. And you will go along the way your chosen teacher leads. There are but two directions you can take, while time remains and choice is meaningful. For never will another road be made except the way to Heaven. You but choose whether to go toward Heaven, or away to nowhere. There is nothing else to choose.
>
> — T-26.V.1.7-12

> How simple is the choice between two things so clearly un-alike.
>
> — T-26.III.7:4

# 2

# IDENTITY
# THEFT

As I read my credit-card statement, my eyes bulged. I was being billed for two $5,000 cash advances I had not taken. Then there was a clothing shopping spree in Dallas. Someone had stolen my credit-card information and gone to town on it. Fortunately, the credit-card company absorbed those losses, but they were not unusual. Every day crooks steal the identities of about 36,000 people, at an annual dollar value of $21 billion. As a result, banks and Internet businesses have elaborate security measures to protect customers' identities.

There is an even more insidious form of identity theft that has hijacked far more than your credit-card account. This theft has caused you to forget who you are and believe that you are small, limited, and powerless—a denial of your true self and an assertion of a false you.

Grand theft identity began soon after you arrived on Earth. Parents, teachers, siblings, clergy, and authority figures told you that you are inept, insignificant, ugly, stupid, unworthy, and sinful, and that the world is a dangerous jungle with threats at every turn. Over time you began to believe these terrible lies, until the day came when you forgot your innate beauty, strength, innocence, and safety. Eventually you adopted an identity contrary to your divine nature and have since lived as someone you are not.

## The Palace and the Fish Market

The story is told of a princess who was kidnapped as a child and taken to live among fishmongers. She grew up amidst piles of fish, smelled like them, and adopted the mentality of a struggling hawker. Years later, one of the king's servants found the princess and brought her back to the royal palace. Her parents welcomed her joyfully and showed her to her elegant room laden with a plush bed, fine linens, colorful flowers, aromatic incense, a breathtaking view, and servants at her beck and call. During her first night in the palace the princess tossed and turned. "Get me out of here," she cried out. "I want to go home."

What the princess did not realize was that she *was* home. Elegance, royalty, and riches were her birthright. But she had gotten so used to living amidst foul smells and poverty that she believed those conditions were her true place in life. *Normal* does not equal *natural*. Like the princess, we have all become accustomed to living in psychic quarters far shabbier than we deserve.

You can find your way back to the palace by remembering your true origin. *A Course in Miracles* urges us to claim, "I am as God created me." Of all the ACIM Workbook Lessons, this one (Lesson 94) is the only one repeated, not just once (Lesson 110) but *twice* (Lesson 162), as well as in many reviews and the Text. The Course is driving home the truth that your real identity is spiritual and spiritual only. You are not your name, age, weight, address, religion, relationship status, job, bank statement, medical diagnosis, or any other attribute by which the world identifies you. While social convention pigeonholes you by fragmented aspects, you remain whole as you were created. The entire *Course in Miracles* is geared to help you regard yourself through the same eyes with which Higher Power recognizes you. When you share that vision, you live in the dignity of your divine identity.

> The journey to God is merely the reawakening of the knowledge of where you are always, and what you are forever.
>
> — T-8.VI.9:6

## She Loves Me, Yeah, Yeah, Yeah

If you tell a lie often enough, you start to believe it. When I was in junior high school, I went to a Beatles concert in Atlantic City. At school the next day, I decided to impress my classmate Donna by telling her that I had met Paul McCartney on his way out of the concert hall. Even more exciting, Paul had given me his guitar pick! To prove it, I showed Donna the pick with his initials "P.M." carved in it. Her pupils dilated. To electrify her further, I placed the pick in her hand and told her I wanted her to have it. Donna swooned and gave me a kiss on the cheek, which made my year. Word got around that I had obtained Paul McCartney's pick, and I had my junior high school day in the sun.

The story, of course, was complete bunk. But I told it so many times over the course of the days that followed, with increasing detail, that now when I think of it, it seems as real as many events that actually happened. I can clearly picture Paul running out the back door of the concert hall and tossing the pick my way. I feel the excitement of an event that never occurred!

Psychologists tell us that the subconscious cannot distinguish between reality and imagination. The images we impress upon our mind, especially when accompanied by emotion, yield the same experience whether they are true or fictional. When hypnotists touch a pencil eraser to a hypnotized person's forearm and tell the person that the eraser is a lit cigarette, the arm blisters. When a lit cigarette is touched to the forearm, but identified as a pencil eraser, no blister develops. ACIM tells us, "The thoughts you hold are mighty, and illusions are as strong in their effects as is the truth" (W-132.1:4). It also explains,

> . . . if you hope to spare yourself from fear there are some things you must realize, and realize fully. The mind is very powerful, and never loses its creative force. It never sleeps. Every instant it is creating. It is hard to recognize that thought and belief combine into a power surge that can

literally move mountains . . . There *are* no idle thoughts. All thinking produces form at some level.

— T-2.VI.9:4-8,13-14

What gives rise to the perception of a whole world can hardly be called idle.

— W-16.2:2

Your subconscious mind has adopted an enormous array of lies about yourself, underscoring what's wrong with you and the world. You have been playing out these untruths in your relationships, career, finances, health, and other significant arenas of your life. The world you see is based on a mass of illusions that *appear* to be real because so many people agree with them and base their lives on them. Yet popularity cannot make fiction true, and habit cannot render fear more substantial than love. The only cure for illusions is truth. The only cure for a mistaken identity is to remember who you are.

## Who Played God?

In the classic film *The Ten Commandments,* Moses, portrayed by Charlton Heston, climbs to the top of Mount Sinai, where he encounters God in the vision of a burning bush. When Moses asks God why He has not heard the prayers of the enslaved Hebrew people, God answers that He has indeed heard their prayers, and He is sending Moses to Pharaoh to deliver the Hebrew nation from bondage.

"Who am I, Lord, that You should send me?" asks Moses.

"I wilt teach thee what thou wilt say," God answers. Moses then beseeches God to reveal His name. God replies, "I am that I am."

For many years, the identity of the actor who spoke the voice of God was kept secret. Eventually it was revealed that the voice in that scene was that of Charlton Heston, deepened by special effects. The scene, drawn verbatim from the Bible, offers a magnificent spiritual insight: The voice of God is your own voice. When God speaks to you—which occurs every moment, whether or not you are aware of it—you are receiving guidance from your own Self. The special effects of the illusory world have distorted your voice to make you think it is that of another, and the studio has kept the process under wraps. But eventually secrets give way to truth. When you talk to God, you are having a conversation with yourself. The "I am" that you are is the "I am" that God is.

When you challenge God as to how the world will be changed, His answer is: *through you*. This does not mean you need to literally take up a staff, confront Pharaoh, and free an oppressed nation. (Although, metaphorically speaking, that is precisely what you are to do.) It means, more fundamentally, that your world will be liberated when you bring the presence of God to the world simply by being yourself. What saves you, along with the world, is your own true Self.

## The Invasion of the Soul Snatchers

When my friend Sara visited a hospital to see her friend's newborn baby, she found the maternity ward locked down, under heavy security. A few months earlier someone had sneaked into the ward and stolen a baby. Since that incident, the hospital made sure it didn't happen again. The event is symbolic of what happened to all of us. Fear and illusion snatched us from our true family. We were taken, as the Bible describes, to "a far country," where truth was twisted so radically that hell seems to be the lot of humanity, escaped by but a scant few saintly souls.

Yet, like the prodigal son, at some point we get fed up with groveling in the mud with pigs. We sense that the life we are living can't be the one God intended for us, and we grow restless to find our way home. When our life becomes empty and burdensome, we reach for higher answers. Then someone tells us about *A Course in Miracles* or another valuable teaching that serves as a spiritual GPS to map our way home. We have delved as far as we can into the world of illusion and we are hungry for the truth. And as we ask, so it is given.

> Be not content with littleness . . . Yet what you do not realize, each time you choose, is that your choice is your evaluation of yourself. Choose littleness and you will not have peace, for you will have judged yourself unworthy of it . . . It is essential that you accept the fact, and accept it gladly, that there is no form of littleness that can ever content you . . . For you will be content only in magnitude . . .

> — EXCERPTED FROM T-15.III.1-2

# 3

# GET REAL

Sitting backstage at a network television studio in a large metropolitan city, I waited to go on the air for an interview. My segment was scheduled right after the noon news broadcast, which began with a gory account of a murder, then a rape, then war footage, followed by bad economic news and a political scandal. I began to feel depressed, but consoled myself that the broadcast would get to more positive reports. It didn't. The entire 15 minutes was filled with gloom and doom, nothing anyone in their right mind would want to wake up in the morning and face. Eventually I just had to laugh. The news was *beyond* depressing. It was *ridiculous*. It was *unbelievable*. Finally, after the closing sortie of auto accidents and snarled traffic, the newscaster announced, ". . . and now for an inspiring new book by an author who is going to tell you how to live a meaningful life."

The camera turned to me.

Suddenly I became Neo in the movie *The Matrix,* where the mysterious Morpheus extends two open hands, a red pill in one palm and a blue pill in the other. If Neo ingests the red pill, he will awaken to his true self and the real world. If he takes the blue pill, he will remain in a familiar but oppressive world of illusions.

I sat up straight and reached for the red pill. I told the audience that well-being is our birthright and fear the impostor. I took a stand for living authentically in a world fallen prey to illusions. I gave a different account of the news from the one that preceded me. I told the viewers that they deserved better than the world has taught them, and that they held power over their lives regardless of the insanity surrounding them. It was the only news I knew how to broadcast.

After the program, the anchor, a highly respected, lifelong journalist, took me aside and told me, "I agree with you completely. I get depressed coming to this job. There has to be more to life and the world than we are telling people there is."

> If you could accept the world as meaningless and let the truth be written upon it for you, it would make you indescribably happy.

> — W-12.5:3

## Heat Up Your Dreams

We've all had people throw cold water on our hot dreams. You told a friend or relative about the person you wished to marry, the business you planned to launch, or the exotic cruise you were thinking about signing up for. But instead of the "Go for it!" you hoped to hear, you heard a snooty "Get real!" Instantly your excitement was reduced to ashes and you either gave up your quest or you had to work to once again build up the courage and momentum to forge ahead. "Cast not pearls before swine" (Matthew 7:6).

When others attempt to gobble your hopes in the shredder of doubt, Higher Power stands with you. "'Who walks with me?' This question should be asked a thousand times a day, till certainty has ended doubting and established peace" (W-156.8:1–2). When the world does not understand, accept, or support you, you do not walk alone. And if you should lose faith in yourself, God still has faith in you.

When most people say "Get real," they mean *Get small. Get limited. Get stuck. I am trapped in my little fear-bound world, and your expansive vision is threatening to me. So I demand that you grovel in the mud with me. How dare you rock my tiny world with greater possibilities!* The premise is that success and happiness are unattainable illusions, while struggle and suffering are realities we must live with. And misery *does* love company.

*A Course in Miracles* has another idea. It tells us, "Nothing the world believes is true" (W-139.7:1), and asks us to remember, "I am entitled to miracles" (W, Lesson 77). Happiness, well-being, and success are your birthright and your destiny. All else is a trick of the mind. The Course tells us that everything the world believes is inside out and upside down, like a photographic negative that makes white seem black and black seem white. Photographic negatives make no sense and they look creepy. So does the world. "Fear is that little darkroom where negatives are developed," said actor and speaker Michael Pritchard.

When minds are given to illusion, fear ascends to the throne of humanity. Yet, "I am at home. Fear is the stranger here" (W, Lesson 160). If you want to know what is true, take what you have been taught about the way life is, and reverse it. Only then will you glimpse reality. As the character Valentine in Tom Stoppard's play *Arcadia* said, "It's the best possible time to be alive, when almost everything you thought you knew is wrong!"

## That's So Fake!

As a kid I used to go to the movies with my buddies every Saturday afternoon and sit through two or three showings of monster films. There would always come a scene in which the gigantic dinosaur was about to devour the explorer. In those days special effects were primitive, and it was obvious that the dinosaur was really a four-inch lizard the cameraman found in his back yard and zoomed in on for an extreme close-up. At that point one of my friends would elbow me and say, laughing, "That's so fake!"

*A Course in Miracles* is your buddy sitting next to you when the monster comes on the screen of the movie of life. The Course elbows you, laughs, and reminds you, "That's so fake!"

> You can indeed afford to laugh at fear thoughts, remembering that God goes with you wherever you go.
>
> — W-41.10:1

No matter how real the special effects of the world *seem*, they are a movie nevertheless and deserve no more credence than the ones you see in a theater. Albert Einstein is said to have noted, "Reality is an illusion, albeit a persistent one."

## God Did Not Create a Meaningless World

The Course calls us to distinguish between the real world that God created and the illusory world that fear has manufactured. Workbook Lesson 14 tells us, "God did not create a meaningless world." The Lesson asks us to affirm, "God did not create that disaster, and so it is not real" (W-14.4:7). It then asks us to consider other frightening events we observe, and affirm for each one, "God did not create that [_____], and so it is not real." The Lesson underscores, "The world you see has nothing to do with reality" (W-14.1:4). The Course is training us to withdraw the credibility we have attributed to events that do not spring from truth.

*Now wait a minute!* the reasoning mind retorts. *Those events <u>are</u> real. They happen every day. I know people they have happened to. Don't stick your head in the sand of denial and argue that disasters are not real. They are!*

The Course sees sorrowful experiences from a different viewpoint. It tells us that when we become upset over fearsome events and give them undue power, we are sticking our heads in the sand as we deny the presence of love. This is a radical departure from the way we have been taught to see the world. But if you wish to change your life radically, a radical departure is required. If your life is working perfectly and you are happy, then carry on. If, on the other hand, your current reality is not bringing you the peace you crave, it may be time to consider another way of looking at life. Maybe you need a miracle. Maybe you need an entire course in miracles. Maybe we all do.

## When Great Spirits Get Real

When Hay House Radio (www.hayhouseradio.com) invited me to host a weekly show, I had to come up with a title for the program. Immediately the name *Get Real* came to me. I like it because it is a double entendre. At first glance, it is an invitation to be honest about who you are, what you believe, and how you want to live—a call to walk authentically. More deeply I seek to remind listeners that who they are is far more real than the world has taught them. We are each an expression of God, a holy idea breathed into existence. We are the divine falling in love with itself. We are spiritual beings created in the image and likeness of a beneficent Creator. "What He creates is not apart from Him, and nowhere does the Father end, the Son begin as something separate from Him" (W-132.12:4).

Most of the people who have changed the world for the better were told, "Get real." The most brilliant agents of positive change have been branded insane, shamed, imprisoned, tortured, and killed. Einstein noted, "Great spirits have always encountered violent opposition from mediocre minds." Jonathan Swift declared, "When a true genius appears, you can know him by this sign: that all the dunces are in a confederacy against him." The Catholic Church kept Galileo under house arrest until his death because he suggested that the earth revolved around the sun. Around the same time, Italian philosopher Giordano Bruno suggested that the universe contains an infinite number of inhabited worlds populated by other intelligent beings. Giordano was convicted of heresy and burned at the stake. When the judges issued his death decree, Bruno answered, "Perchance you who pronounce my sentence are in greater fear than I who receive it."

Inventor Thomas Edison engaged in a vehement campaign to stop visionary scientist Nikola Tesla from proliferating alternating current (AC) electricity. Edison wanted the world to depend on his discovery, direct current (DC), and although Tesla's alternating current was far more efficient, Edison would stop at nothing to undermine Tesla, including electrocuting horses in public to demonstrate the "dangers" of the new form of electricity. Edison was telling Tesla, "Get real." Tesla had no choice but to answer, "I already am." Ultimately, truth prevailed. Now, every time you turn on a light, you can thank Nikola Tesla for getting real.

So the next time someone tells you, "Get real," take their advice as the highest compliment. Thank the speaker for reminding you to be who you are and do what you are here to do. Your purpose on Earth goes far beyond satisfying critics or proving yourself according to standards others set for you. Your purpose is to recognize the greatness within you and deliver it. The Chinese philosopher Chuang Tzu said, "The sage dwells among those things that can never be lost, and so he lives forever." Show the world what is real by establishing yourself in *vision*, not *division*. Invite naysayers to meet you on higher ground. They need your reality far more than you need theirs.

> Love waits on welcome, not on time, and the real world is but your welcome of what always was. Therefore the call of joy is in it, and your glad response is your awakening to what you have not lost.
>
> — T-13.VII.9:7-8

## How Did *A Course in Miracles* Come to the World?

The way *A Course in Miracles* came to the world is as miraculous as the teaching it transmits. The way it came *is* the teaching it transmits.

Dr. Helen Schucman and Dr. Bill Thetford were psychologists at Columbia University's College of Physicians and Surgeons. Both were highly respected in their field, and Dr. Thetford also held the position of director of the clinical psychology department at Columbia-Presbyterian Hospital in New York City. As is often typical in academia, the two were not getting along, professionally and personally. They were caught up in competition, backbiting, and ego. After an intense period of acrimony, Bill reached his limit and declared passionately to Helen, "There must be another way." Uncharacteristically, Helen agreed and promised him to help find the better way.

This moment is cited as the seminal interaction that led to the birth of *A Course in Miracles*. Two people who had been steeped in separation chose to join. With that spark of willingness, a door opened through which came a teaching that would significantly uplift humanity.

Soon after that conversation, Helen began to hear an inner voice, which, she explained, was like "strong and compelling thought impressions." It told her, "This is a course in miracles. Please take notes." She was disturbed by this event since, as a psychologist, she knew that people who heard voices were often judged mentally ill.

Dr. Schucman reluctantly told Dr. Thetford, "Bill, I have been hearing a voice."

"What does it say?"

"It says, 'This is a course in miracles. Please take notes.' What do you think I should do?"

Bill thought for a few moments and replied, "Why don't you take notes?"

Anxious and resistant, but bolstered by Bill's response, Helen took a stenography pad and recorded what the voice was dictating to her. This introduction came:

> This is a course in miracles. It is a required course. Only the time you take it is voluntary. Free will does not mean that you can establish the curriculum. It means only that you can elect what you want to take at a given time. The course does not aim at teaching the meaning of love, for that is beyond what can be taught. It does aim, however, at removing the blocks to the awareness of love's presence, which is your natural inheritance. The opposite of love is fear, but what is all-encompassing can have no opposite.
>
> — T-In.1.1-8

When Helen showed Bill the content, he was moved. He told her he thought the material was extraordinary, and he encouraged her to keep taking notes.

Soon Helen and Bill established a ritual as partners in scribing *A Course in Miracles*. Helen went into Bill's office early each morning, steno pad in hand. He pulled down the blinds, and she read what she had recorded. A skilled typist, Bill set Helen's reading to paper. This process went on for seven years.

Soon thereafter the scribes, joined by their colleague and co-editor Dr. Kenneth Wapnick, connected via a series of uncanny synchronicities with Judy Skutch (Whitson). Together with Judy's husband, Bob Skutch, they formed the nonprofit Foundation for Inner Peace, which published the first edition of *A Course in Miracles* in 1976.

The publisher has never invested in advertising or marketing, relying strictly on word of mouth to proliferate the Course. To date, the Course has sold over three million copies, translated into 25 languages, and continues to grow in popularity and respect, transforming lives in the most profound ways.

# 4

# LIGHT IN THE
# THEATER

In the early days of motion pictures, a group of cowboys got together in a cabin to watch their first movie, projected onto a sheet on a wall. The movie came to a scene in which a band of war-painted Indians bolted over a rise, hooting and hollering on their rampage to attack a passing cavalry battalion. Upon seeing the ambush, one of the cowboys in the cabin stood, pulled out his pistol, and fired six shots at the war party. The lights in the room came on, and everyone laughed to see six bullet holes in a blank sheet on the wall.

*A Course in Miracles* tells us that, like the movie in the story about the cowboys, the world we see is a projection of our thoughts. The environment *seems* to be populated by people and things that have a life of their own, but it is *we* who breathe life into appearances by our belief in them. Our experience springs, more accurately, from our *in*-vironment. When we fight the outer world, we are the frightened cowboy shooting wildly at a sheet, battling our own projections. When the outer world is kind to us, we are being kind to ourselves, immersed in the projection of our loving thoughts.

Your thoughts are the film, your mind is the projector, and the sheet is the world. You will never find peace by blaming external people and events for your misery, or by giving them credit for your salvation. You are doing it all to and for yourself.

Projection always sees your wishes in others.

— T-7.VII.9:4

19

## A Shaggy Duck Story

When I lived in an organic farming community, one morning I sat on the porch of the bunkhouse, watching members walk across a grassy area to the dining hall. Beside the path, Pete the duck sat and quacked at people as they walked by.

A professional singer was the first to pass by Pete that morning. Upon hearing him, she stopped and told him, "How nice of you to sing me a morning song!"

The next woman along the path was rather overweight. When she heard Pete quack in her direction, she scolded him, "You're always quacking for more food, Pete. It's time you stuck to your diet!"

The final person to pass was a very intellectual architect. Hearing Pete's voice, he retorted, "Questions, Pete—always questions! How about some answers for a change?"

Hmm . . .

Each person saw Pete through the lens of his or her own self-perception. They projected their worldview onto the duck and attributed their beliefs about themselves to him. It was their own selves they were talking to. We are all speaking only to our own self.


## Projection to Get Rid of Guilt

A telling biblical account (Leviticus 16:20–22) gives us a keen insight into how we use projection as a psychological defense mechanism to divest ourselves of guilt. When the newly birthed Hebrew nation was wandering in the wilderness searching for the Promised Land, the people grew discouraged. Some believed that their sins were preventing them from reaching their destination. So the priest Aaron brought a goat to the center of the camp and told the people to cast their sins into the beast. After they followed his instruction, the goat was driven out of the camp into the desert, taking with it, they believed, their sins. This is the origin of the word *scapegoat.*

Not much has changed in the 5,000 years since that ritual was conducted. We still believe we can rid ourselves of our unwanted traits by projecting them onto other people. Ex-spouses serve as excellent candidates for projection, as do ethnic and racial groups. Hitler and the German nation used the Jewish people to scapegoat their mass disowned shadow. Crusades and inquisitions have murdered millions in the name of Christ. Witch hunts, literal and political, have burned countless innocent people at the stake. Women have been beaten and downtrodden for centuries. African Americans have been incarcerated for decades for crimes they didn't commit. Gays have been denied rights and ostracized . . . And on and on. The relief the ego promises via projection results only in tragedy.

No one can draw a cloak of darkness over the outer world and retain awareness of inner light. Projection promises to protect the self, but it only disempowers. Your true self, ACIM assures you, needs no protection. "In my defenselessness my safety lies" (W, Lesson 153). Who you are is eternal, invulnerable, and without sin. Projection will only deepen the rift you perceive between yourself and love. You do not need to get rid of what you never had. When you release others from the projection of your false assumed weakness, you release yourself.

## The Birth of a Wrathful God

The ultimate disowned shadow self is the projection of anger onto God. Wrath is entirely a human experience, incited by a sense of guilt, fear, powerlessness, and separation. None of these traits belong to God. All the scary tales you have heard about an angry, punitive God are the result of anthropomorphizing divinity with disowned humanity. As French philosopher Voltaire aptly stated, "God created us in His image and likeness, and we returned the compliment."

Whenever there is a natural disaster, someone claims it to be a punishment from God. After the 2010 Haiti earthquake, Reverend Pat Robertson declared that God was punishing the Haitians for making a pact with the devil. He was severely chastised for this unbrotherly comment. After the 2011 Japanese earthquake and tsunami, the governor of Tokyo announced that this evil had befallen the Japanese people because of egoism and populism in Japanese politics. He, too, was taken to task for this pronouncement, and he later retracted the statement.

The immature mind sees God from the viewpoint of a powerless child under the thumb of an oppressive parent. The mature mind recognizes us as offspring of a kind and forgiving God who would not hurt his beloved children any more than we would choose to hurt our own.

## The Savior Syndrome

Projection does not simply disown our shadow. It also disowns our light. We are prone to deny our self-worth and project it onto an external savior. Savior projection occurs in romantic relationships in which you see yourself as empty, lonely, or broken, and you wish, hope, and pray for a dashing knight on a white horse to whisk you away from diapers and credit-card bills and tell you how gorgeous you are, even with stretch marks. Or you fantasize that the Playmate of the Month will show up at your man cave despite your growing paunch. As "Cinderella-like" as these visions sound, we indulge them. An endless array of romance novels, movies, and songs are based on them. Saviors sell.

The manufacture of religious saviors operates on the same paradigm. "I am lost and in hell or on my way there. You are perfect and you can redeem me. Please save me." Metaphysically, this paradigm includes a true premise: You acknowledge you are in pain, your ego's attempts at salvation have failed, and you desire a way out. You need help, and you are willing to ask for it and receive it. That's smart. *How* you get out of pain and get saved makes all the difference in whether your method of salvation will free you or bind you.

Any savior you project to be outside yourself denies the God within you. This is the meaning of the Buddhist maxim "If you meet the Buddha on the road, kill him." The Buddha is not a person. Like the Christ, Buddha is a state of consciousness, the awareness of divinity within you and all around you. If you limit holiness to one body or personality and you define all other beings as less than divine, you are fabricating a god that is less than God. In *A Course in Miracles,* Jesus repeatedly affirms our equality with him. He identifies himself not as more godly than we are, but as an elder brother who has gone ahead of us on the path we all share, and who extends a helping hand for us to walk beside him. He does not seek our worship. He seeks our *worthship.*

You are not separate from perfection. Buddha asked, "If you do not get it from yourself, where will you go for it?" All journeys outward ultimately lead to the journey inward, where everything you seek already exists and awaits your joyous acceptance.

> Do not be afraid to look within . . . Within you is the holy sign of perfect faith your Father has in you . . . Look, then, upon the light He placed within you, and learn that what you feared was there has been replaced with love.
>
> — T-13.IX.8:1,7,13

## Healing Your Intimate Relationship

Intimate relationships are the arena most susceptible to projection. We see traits in our partner, for better and worse, that we have disowned from ourselves. Then we worship the other person at the expense of our own dignity, or we attack the other person, mirroring our battle with ourselves.

Meanwhile you are equal to your partner in value, beauty, wisdom, and strength. You have made up a story about who your partner is. If it's a good story, stick with it. If the story is causing you pain, get a new one. If you are tempted to fight or idolize your partner, remember that no person has the power to hurt you or save you. Only you can hurt or save yourself. Release your partner from your projections and you will recognize both of you as divine beings so brilliant in light that you could hardly look upon one another. Then you will have the relationship your heart desires.

ACIM refers to our relationship partners as our saviors—but not in the way we have been taught to believe that someone will save us. Our partner becomes our savior when we choose to see the light in him and love him for who he is, not who we want to change him to be. Likewise when we accept her as a complete and radiant soul, even if she doesn't match a cover-girl image. Thus we are saved from our illusions and projections and we create a relationship with the person God created, not the story we made up about him or her.

## Authority Figurines

One of the most prevalent projection errors is the projection of authority onto external sources. You believe there are people and groups outside of you that have power over you: spouses, parents, landlords, neighbors, bosses, corporations, governments, and religions, to name a few. *There are no external sources.* The source of your experience with these "others" is your mind.

> Ideas leave not their source . . . What is projected out, and seems to be external to the mind, is not outside at all, but an effect of what is in . . .
>
> —T-26.VII.4:7,9

Authority figures are really authority *figurines*, animated by the power you have attributed to them. Just as you have invested that power, you can withdraw it. No one and no thing has power over your soul, and neither do they deserve it. It is tempting to complain about how greedy corporations are taking over the world or how the corrupt government is ruining your life. You will find plenty of people to agree with you, which only reinforces the projection and deepens the suffering it generates. Take back the power you have given to authority figurines, and claim the authority of your creations. Then your projections of evil and salvation will wither, and you will not need saving because you already stand on holy ground.

## The Key to Healing Projection

The antidote to projection, ACIM explains, is *extension.* Extension means that we recognize godly attributes within ourselves, and we extend them to enfold the world we perceive outside of us. Extension is similar to projection in that we are taking something inside ourselves and seeing it outside. But in extension we are not fabricating a separation between ourselves and what we see. Instead, we enfold the world in the goodness that abides at the core of our being. Projection splits and disowns. Extension includes and embraces.

ACIM urges us to take back our projections and affirm our extensions. I am not a separate person writing this book to you or for you. You have written this book to and for yourself, through me. I am the agent you have enlisted to remind you of what you already know. My mentor Hilda Charlton once asked me if I wrote *A Course in Miracles.* I had to laugh; her question seemed absurd. *A Course in Miracles* was written by God through Jesus Christ. That's not me. I regarded myself as a humble student, ignorant and struggling, hoping to someday grasp this eloquent, poetic, beyond-this-world material.

Over the years as I have delved deeper into the Course and pondered my mentor's question, I realize there may be more truth to her inquiry than I understood at the time. Spiritual masters do not ask foolish questions. What appears to be a silly question often contains a nugget of genius, revealed later as the student matures. Metaphysically speaking, I *did* write *A Course in Miracles,* and *so did you.* Whatever comes into our field of vision represents our consciousness. "You spot it, you got it." Projection tells us that words of divinity come from outside of us, trying to find their way in. Extension tells us that spiritually powerful ideas arise from inside of us, finding their way out. Ultimately there is no in and out. Everything you can imagine and experience is within you. When projection gives way to extension, you are no longer separate from your creations, and all that you seek, you are.

## The Meaning of Atonement

ACIM speaks often of the "atonement," which many students have a hard time understanding. Atonement is the undoing of the world of fear and the return to love. It is the awakening from the dream of separation, taking back projection, and restoring the condition of wholeness. It is the releasing of the limited identity as body or ego, and the reclaiming of our true identity as Spirit. It is the evaporation of the illusions of sin, loss, and death, and the homecoming to our natural state of peace.

> The Garden of Eden, or the pre-separation condition, was a state of mind in which nothing was needed. When Adam listened to the "lies of the serpent," all he heard was untruth. You do not have to continue to believe what is not true unless you choose to do so. All that can literally disappear in the twinkling of an eye because it is merely a misperception.
>
> — T-2.I.3:1-4

The atonement is the twinkling of an eye in which misperception gives way to the real world. Heaven has been here all the time; we just weren't seeing it. When you are tired of seeing a pained and tormented world, you will see a healed world. Then the atonement will be accomplished.

We all project, and we live in the world of our projections. To be in a body is to perceive people and things as separate from you. Yet the dynamic of projection is not cause for despair, but celebration. God so loves and trusts you that He gave you the power to conjure entire worlds and explore them. The power of the *Star Trek* holodeck is minuscule compared to the infinite universes you and I weave with our thoughts. Yet the time comes when you say, as the captain of the *Enterprise* commanded, "Computer: Game over." At that moment, the 3-D illusions disappear and you find yourself standing before a blank screen.

Until then, practice extending thoughts that create the world you would choose rather than the one handed you by default. Until the images all dissolve into light, it's the best game in town.

> There is no world apart from what you wish, and herein lies your ultimate release. Change but your mind on what you want to see, and all the world must change accordingly.
>
> — W-132.5:1-2

# 5

# THE SIN THAT HAD NO EFFECT

While presenting a program in Spokane, Washington, I connected with my friend Alden Crull, a dedicated ACIM student. Alden didn't just talk the Course. He *lived* it. One day when I needed a ride to a meeting, Alden kindly offered to drive me. Before I was to meet him, I had a massage, during which I fell asleep, and I woke up after the time we had agreed to meet. When I finally arrived at our meeting point, Alden had given up waiting and gone home. I felt terrible about making him wait and missing my appointment with him.

When I saw Alden the next day, I told him, "I'm so sorry I inconvenienced you." Then I waited for his punitive response. But it never came. Instead, Alden smiled and told me, "No problem. Would you like a ride anywhere today?"

Alden's response reversed the laws of the world and applied instead the law of miracles. According to a worldly mind-set, someone who had been stood up would be offended and say, "The heck with you. I'm not going to put myself out again, only to be let down. Find your own ride." But Alden took an altogether different approach. He demonstrated to me that what I believed was my sin that had hurt him, actually had not. He was a true teacher of God.

Alden modeled ACIM's formula for healing: Show others that their *perceived* sins have had no effect on you. "Your mission is very simple. You are asked to live so as to demonstrate that you are not an ego . . ." (T-4.VI.6:2–3). Prove that you are deeper, richer, and stronger than any apparently foolish, unconscious, or evil behavior someone acts out. Simultaneously affirm that the sins you *perceive* you have committed against others have not harmed them.

29

All the results of sin, against ourselves or others, are simply a story we have fabricated. We keep sin alive by practicing its adverse effects. When we practice that sin has no effect, we free ourselves and others. "What has no effect does not exist, and to the Holy Spirit the effects of error are nonexistent" (T-9.IV.5:5).

## The Ego Strikes Back

"But that person's wrongdoing really *did* hurt me!" the ego argues. "I lost my well-deserved promotion because my co-worker manipulated my supervisor for the position." "Someone infected me with a sexually transmitted disease." "The government uses my hard-earned tax money to wage war and keep able people on welfare."

You further attest to the reality of sin and its effects when you feel guilty for the pain or sorrow you believe you have caused others. "I screwed up my child because I was an alcoholic." "When I cheated on my husband, I caused him irreparable pain." "My parents paid for my college education so I could become a doctor, and now I feel awful because all I want to do is be an actor."

We have all felt hurt by plenty of people and incidents, and we all feel guilty about hurting others. While all of these sufferings seem very real and justifiable, *A Course in Miracles* teaches that your true Self, and the true Self of any other person, runs far deeper than the self that experiences pain. "Whatever suffers is not part of me" (W, Lesson 248). No matter what mistakes you have made or others have made against you, your inner being remains perfectly intact, impervious to human error. It was not the act that hurt, but *your interpretation* of the act. Just as you chose an interpretation that hurts, you can choose one that heals. "I can elect to change all thoughts that hurt" (W, Lesson 284).

## In the Image of Love

ACIM assures us that there is nothing you could do that could cause you to lose the grace of God, force life to punish you, or require you to suffer in any way. No matter what bleak identity or obligation the world lays over you, you are innocent, absolutely lovable, and deserving of only good. You remain as God created you.

> Holiness created me holy.
> Kindness created me kind.
> Helpfulness created me helpful.
> Perfection created me perfect.
>
> — W-67.2:3-6

> Love, which created me, is what I am.
>
> — W, Lesson 229

To be healed and happy you must seek, find, and affirm evidence for your innocence. If this seems difficult, recognize that you have become adept at seeking, finding, and affirming signs of your guilt. You are a master at selecting elements of your experience and using them to prove your weakness. You can use the same faculty of selective perception to underscore your strength. Tip the balance of justice in your favor by realizing that the only real justice is forgiveness.

ACIM regards sin as a meaningless fiction without cause or effect, a fantasy with no basis in reality. It asks you to forgive your brother for what he *didn't* do, and overlook the "never done" (W-99.4:3). Release your brother and yourself from the illusion that his actions can determine your experience. No one has the power to rob your happiness, unless you give that power to them. No one can drive you crazy unless you accept the passenger's seat. *A Course in Miracles* shows us how to take our power back and drive rather than being driven.

## Only Blessings Remain

All sin lurks in the darkened halls of the past. It is your *thoughts* about what happened in the past that make sins, both yours and others', seem so formidable. When you live in the present moment, sin is a nonentity. It is meaningless. It doesn't exist. The key to overcoming sin is to *change your thoughts about the past* so they do not encroach on the holy present moment.

During my high school years, I walked to school every morning with my buddy George. One day, as a spontaneous act of affection, I reached my arm around George's shoulder. My friend was uncomfortable with this gesture and he pushed my arm away. Sensing I had invaded his space, I felt embarrassed. We both said nothing and just kept walking. Later that year we headed off to college and went our separate ways. For a long time, however, when I thought about George, I recalled that awkward moment and I cringed at the memory.

One morning decades later my office assistant told me, "Someone named George called. He found you on the Internet. He says he misses you and wishes he could walk to school with you again."

Astonished, I phoned George and we made an appointment to meet. Over lunch we began to reminisce. "I know this sounds weird," I told him, "but sometimes I still feel awkward about the morning I put my arm around your shoulder and you tossed it off."

George looked perplexed. "I don't remember that at all," he told me. "All I remember is that you waited for me every morning, even in the rain."

I was stunned. For all those years, one of my primary memories of my friendship with George was my perceived error. Meanwhile, all he remembered was the good. The only place that painful memory existed in the entire universe was in my mind. What a waste of my thoughts and energy! How comforting it felt to know that George had always appreciated me. I decided to choose *his* memory of me rather than the one I had been carrying for so many years. Therein came my freedom.

"But what if George did not forgive you?" ego jumps in and asks. "What if he had felt embarrassed by that act, or hurt by a more serious one, and he resented you and refused to talk to you for the rest of your life? What if you both went to your graves angry at each other and brokenhearted?" (Ego has a way of dramatizing scenarios, you may have noticed.)

George had a choice about how he regarded that event. He chose to not even notice it, or just to forget about it. It was *my* mind that held on to it, so I was the one who suffered.

When you *seem* to commit a sin against someone, there are two parts to the equation: (1) what you did, and (2) how that person thinks about it. What you did is simply an act, without any inherent meaning. "I have given everything I see . . . all the meaning that it has for me" (W, Lesson 2). How that person thinks about the act determines her experience of it. If she chooses to feel hurt, angry, or resentful, that is the experience she will live in. If she chooses to forget about it or dwell instead on appreciative memories, she will live in *that* experience. You are responsible for your action, but the other person is responsible for her interpretation of your action and her subsequent experience.

You have had billions of moments of experiences. The moments you give your attention to are the ones that generate your current experience. When you focus on painful memories, you create a painful past and drag it into the present. When you focus on joyful memories, you create a joyful past and experience peace in the present moment.

A coaching client told me, "I am haunted by my past."

I told him, "Your past has no power to haunt you. You are haunting yourself by focusing on a past that hurts."

You heal a haunting past by giving your attention instead to a blessing past. ACIM calls us to affirm, "The past is over. It can touch me not" (W, Lesson 289), and reminds us, "All your past except its beauty is gone, and nothing is left but a blessing" (T-5. IV.8:2).

> I have saved all your kindnesses and every loving thought you ever had. I have purified them of the errors that hid their light, and kept them for you in their own perfect radiance. They are beyond destruction and beyond guilt

. . . You can indeed depart in peace because I have loved you as I loved myself. You go with my blessing and for my blessing. Hold it and share it, that it may always be ours.

—T-5.IV.8:3-5,7-9

## God Has Memory Issues

A story is told about a woman named Maria who was reputed to speak with Jesus regularly. A sour old priest heard about Maria and sought to discredit her. He went to Maria and told her, "I heard that you talk to Jesus."

"That's right."

"Then the next time you talk to Jesus, would you ask him what was the sin I committed when I was in the seminary?"

"I will ask him," Maria replied. "Come back in a week and I will tell you what he said."

The priest departed, smug that he had foiled the impostor's ruse.

A week later the priest returned and asked Maria, "Did you speak with Jesus this week?"

"Yes, I did."

"Did you ask him what was the sin I committed when I was in the seminary?"

"I did."

"And what did Jesus say?" The priest sat back, arms crossed.

"He said, 'I forgot.'"

God has no memory of our sins because He was never aware of them in the first place. "God does not forgive because He never has condemned" (W-46.1:1). Forgiveness is required only by those who have condemned. If condemnation has not entered your consciousness, forgiveness is meaningless and unnecessary. The Course describes forgiveness as the final illusion that undoes all the illusions that preceded it. If we wish to be like God and experience the deep soul satisfaction that godly beings enjoy, we need to sharpen our forgetting skills.

## *Your Future Isn't What It Used to Be*

The future you expect is a projection of your beliefs about the past. The future will be like the past only if you keep thinking the same thoughts that created the past. When you change your thoughts about the past, you change your thoughts about the future, and thus you create a better future. Your future, like your past, is a story you have made up. If you regard yourself and life through the lens of fear, guilt, and mistrust, you will expect a morbid future. If you regard yourself and life through the lens of love, innocence, and faith, you will expect a bright future. If you fear what is to come, you have succumbed to a belief in sin. *A Course in Miracles* assures us that we will not be punished for our sins because we don't have any. It tells us plainly, ". . . all that you believe must come from sin will never happen" (W-101.5:2).

The ego is obsessed with planning because it believes that if it doesn't control everything, something terrible will happen. But the exact opposite is true. If the ego doesn't control everything, something *wonderful* will happen. Ironically, it is the ego's preoccupation with control that keeps something wonderful from happening. More accurately, the ego's preoccupation with control keeps you unaware that something wonderful is *already* happening.

ACIM tells us that the only correct expectation of the future is one of limitless good. The Holy Spirit, the Voice for God within us, eagerly anticipates the future as benevolent and blessed.

> [The mind that plans] does not see that here and now is everything it needs to guarantee a future quite unlike the past, without a continuity of any old ideas and sick beliefs. Anticipation plays no part at all, for present confidence directs the way.
>
> — W-135.16:4-5

You don't have to worry about the future. You never did and you never will. The future will take care of itself. "I place the future in the hands of God" (W, Lesson 194). Your job is to establish your consciousness in the wonder, beauty, and value of the

35

present moment, which will make you happy now and keep you happy then.

## No Other Shoe

Many people tense up when things start to get good in their lives. They are "waiting for the other shoe to drop." The idea is that if you get too happy, someone or something will come along and cut you down. This belief is one of the ego's favorite ploys. The ego is threatened by happiness because it believes that if you got too happy, it would be out of a job. So it seeks ways to drag you down if you begin to step out of misery.

*There is no other shoe.* Well-being is your natural state and all you deserve. The Course implores you to remember, "God's Will for me is perfect happiness" (W, Lesson 101). Fear and pain, not joy, are the anomalies. Here we find another example of how the thinking of the world turns truth inside out and upside down. Wellness is your nature and your destiny. All else is the product of twisted thinking.

Guilt is punishing yourself before God doesn't. It is an unnecessary prepayment of retribution for wrongdoing. As a child you were taught that pain buys you freedom. You drew on the wall with crayons, your father spanked you, and your "sin" was paid off. You got a bad grade, you were grounded, and the account was settled. You confessed your sins to a priest, he gave you penance, and you were back in good standing with the Lord. As an adult you got a speeding ticket, you paid a fine, and once again you were "fine." Here's the belief in a nutshell: Sin is offset by pain, which leads to freedom. So now when you believe you have sinned, you beat yourself up and mete out your own punishment before God gives you a worse dose. "The ego believes that by punishing itself it will mitigate the punishment of God" (T-5.V.5:6). But there is no worse dose to come. You did it all to yourself.

You have also learned how good it feels when punishment is over. The contrast between pain and relief from pain can be exhilarating. This is the payoff behind make-up sex. But you don't need pain to enjoy feeling good and you don't need to fight first to enjoy sex. If you keep hitting your head with a hammer, it feels good when you stop, but you could have felt good without the hammer beating. Contrast is a helpful teacher, but after a point it becomes a vicious taskmaster. There are easier ways to learn.

When you feel guilty, you are doing time for imaginary crimes. God takes no pleasure in your pain and doesn't punish you. Neither need you. It's time to stop hurting ourselves.

## Case Dismissed

From the time you were a little child, you were graded, evaluated, rated, compared, and judged on nearly everything you did, and urged to judge others. Life became an endless contest for the best grades, the top team, the highest sales, the richest income, the sexiest body, the most elegant wardrobe, the most Facebook likes, the biggest house, the newest car, and the office with the most windows. Wherever you turn, you find competition, ranking, winners, and losers. Unless your team wins the pennant, you are the top producer, or you win the beauty contest, you have failed. Second place, even by one thousandth of an Olympic second, is not good enough. Mark Twain reportedly said, "Comparison is the death of joy." No wonder so many people are neurotic!

*A Course in Miracles* wipes out all of this insanity. It assures us that who we are as spiritual beings is far beyond judgment. In the eyes of God, you are perfect. All the things for which you believe you deserve condemnation or deem yourself a failure are meaningless. Your wholeness is intact, and your worthiness was never in question. You do not have to compete to prove yourself, for you have unique gifts that no one else can deliver. The judgment you have been running from will never come.

You need not fear the Higher Court will condemn you. It will merely dismiss the case against you. There can be no case against a child of God, and every witness to guilt in God's creations is bearing false witness to God Himself. Appeal everything you believe gladly to God's Own Higher Court, because it speaks for Him and therefore speaks truly. It will dismiss the case against you, however carefully you have built it up. The case may be fool-proof, but it is not God-proof. The Holy Spirit will not hear it, because He can only witness truly. His verdict will always be "thine is the Kingdom," because He was given to you to remind you of what you are.

— T-5.VI.10:1-8

## Real Correction

Does the unreality of sin mean that we should open all the prison doors and set criminals free? Should everyone be allowed to do whatever they want without penalty or punishment? Are we to condone evil? Must we let people hurt us?

Of course not. We do not help people who inflict pain by letting them continue. People who hurt others are hurting themselves. They are disconnected from love. "Hurt people hurt people," as the adage says. To put up with abuse is to abuse yourself as well as the abuser. Where appropriate, we must set boundaries, say no to offensive behavior, and stop criminals.

*How* we stop criminals is the crucial element in preventing aberrant behavior. There are ways to deal with criminals that minimize the likelihood of them repeating their misdeeds. To begin, we must reframe crime as a call for love. ACIM tells us that every act is either an expression of love or a call for love. Anyone who steals, rapes, or murders has a gaping hole in his soul. He feels empty, broken, lost, powerless, and alone. No one connected to his true Self would think of hurting someone else. So while crime is ostensibly a police issue, it is more fundamentally a wounded-soul issue.

The documentary film *The Dhamma Brothers* chronicles the spiritual evolution of a group of life-sentenced prisoners who participated in a Vipassana meditation program. Over time, these hardened offenders used meditation to soothe their tattered souls. They came to greater peace with themselves, each other, and their lives. Their stunning transformation demonstrates that connection with our spiritual Source bears life-changing practical effects.

On a broader scale, studies indicate that when one percent of people in a city meditate regularly, the violent crime rate in that city drops. In 1993 a large group of meditators went to Washington, D.C., known as the murder capital of the nation, to establish greater peace in that city. Soon thereafter the murder rate declined. More than 200 similar experiments have been conducted in schools and prisons around the world, with astounding results. When meditation practices were introduced into prison programs in the country of Senegal, two penitentiaries were ultimately closed. (For a brief overview of this phenomenon, watch "The Square Root of One Percent" on YouTube.)

Prisons achieve containment but not correction. Incarceration keeps potentially dangerous people off the streets, but, as the recidivism rate indicates, it does not rehabilitate them. How, then, does real correction occur?

ACIM tells us that the place to begin all correction is within our own consciousness. While it is important to examine the ways your acts have caused pain to others, it is even more important to examine the pain that has caused you to commit those acts. When you are free of pain, you are incapable of inflicting pain. Thus we heal suffering at its root, not its symptoms. All societal healing begins with self-healing.

It is tempting to try to fix other people rather than face and heal our own fears and judgments. When you accept your own innocence, you will know precisely how to deal with difficult people. Under the cloud of judgment, you cannot see anyone clearly. "Without forgiveness I will still be blind" (W, Lesson 247). As you establish yourself on higher ground, you gain the leverage to lift those who are trapped. "The sole responsibility of the miracle worker is to accept the Atonement for himself" (T-2.V.5:1). Don't wait for others to get their act together before you do. Your act will influence theirs.

Inner peace is your strongest platform to create global transformation. Mahatma Gandhi, Martin Luther King, Jr., and Mother Teresa never made evil their enemy. They didn't fight people. Instead, they made a stand for kindness and equality, and subsequently advanced society in ways that angry people could never achieve. For them, peace was not simply the goal. Peace was the road to all worthy goals.

## When We Love Like God

Master yogi Paramahansa Yogananda encountered a vehement fundamentalist who argued that all bad people should go to hell, and will. Yogananda asked him, "Do you have any children?"

"I have a son," the man answered.

"Does he have any bad habits?"

"Sometimes he comes home drunk."

"Then the next time he comes home drunk, place his head in the oven, turn up the heat as high as you can, and make him stay there forever," Yogananda suggested.

"I would never do that!" the man retorted.

"Why not?"

"Because I love him."

"Then if you, even with your human frailties, love your son so much that you would never punish him so severely, then imagine how much more your Heavenly Father loves you and would never take delight in your suffering."

*A Course in Miracles* tells us that guilt, which implies a severance from love, is the only truly impossible scenario in the universe. If sin were real, we would have all cancelled ourselves out of existence a long time ago. The human condition is abysmal. But sin and punishment have no place in a universe founded in love. When you demonstrate to others that the sins they believe they have committed have no effect, you release them from prison along with yourself. If something has no effect, it has no cause, and it might as well not have happened. Ultimately, only love happens.

> Now are we saved indeed. For in God's Hands we rest untroubled, sure that only good can come to us.
>
> —W-194.9:1-2

# 6

# AT YOUR
# HAND I LIVE

In Charles Dickens's classic book *Great Expectations,* we meet Miss Havisham, an elderly spinster who was jilted at the altar many years earlier. Miss Havisham still wears her yellowed wedding gown while the cobwebbed china for her marital feast sits on her dining-room table beside the uneaten wedding cake. Although the woman is only in her 50s, she looks much older after hiding in the shadows for so many years. She is described as a cross between "waxwork and skeleton."

Miss Havisham is the quintessential bearer of a "treasured wound." Her tattered wedding dress and rotting cake serve as lifelong badges of victimhood. Daily she reminds herself of the loss she cannot get beyond, and glorifies it to the world.

"She should just get over it and get on with her life," you say. Of course. Yet, much as we might not like to admit it, there is a Miss Havisham in all of us. We all bear treasured wounds.

*A Course in Miracles* puts it thus:

> A sick and suffering you but represents your brother's guilt; the witness that you send lest he forget the injuries he gave, from which you swear he never will escape. This sick and sorry picture *you* accept, if only it can serve to punish him. The sick are merciless to everyone . . . if they can say, "Behold me, brother, at your hand I die." For sickness is the witness to his guilt, and death would prove his errors must be sins. Sickness is but a "little" death; a form of vengeance not yet total. Yet it speaks with certainty for what it represents. The bleak and bitter

picture you have sent your brother *you* have looked upon in grief. And everything that it has shown to him have you believed, because it witnessed to the guilt in him which you perceived and loved.

— T-27.I.4:3-11

## The Bloody Robe

The Chinese film *Dream Lovers* offers a dramatic image of how we exalt pain. A man named Song Yu leaves his girlfriend, Wah-Lei, for another woman he believes to be his soul mate. Devastated, Wah-Lei goes to Song Yu's apartment building, slits her wrists, and knocks on his door. When he opens the door he finds her standing in her white robe, arms extended as if on a crucifix, blood dripping to the floor as she moans, "Song Yu!" and collapses to her death.

While the poor girl's act is extreme, she depicts a dynamic we have all played out. If you have ever carried any pain over lost love or betrayal of any kind, you are the jilted lover, wrists slit, blood dripping, falling to your grave as you declare in word or deed, "Behold me, brother, at your hand I die."

*A Course in Miracles* doesn't limit psychic self-mutilation to unrequited love. The Course tells us that *any* illness and *any* pain, physical or emotional, is our way of holding someone else guilty for hurting us. If we did not blame others, the Course explains, we would never be sick.

I realize that this dynamic is a lot to swallow, and you may be tempted to slam this book shut and reach for a bar of Belgian chocolate or a beer. But hang in there and I'll show you how this principle can save your life.

## Body Speaks for Mind

The first step to undoing pain or illness is to identify the *perceived* source of your suffering or loss. This takes extreme honesty, since most people believe that stuff just happens to them from external sources and forces more powerful than they are. Germs jump on you from doorknobs, the flu is "going around," Mercury is in retrograde, Leos are lost without an audience, the wealthy 1 percent is ripping off the disenfranchised 99 percent, karma from a past life has come around to batter you, core programming from dysfunctional parents keeps you downtrodden, or you just plain have bad luck. *A Course in Miracles* would say that all of these "causes" are not causes at all. Mind is the only cause, and body is the effect. "I am affected only by my thoughts" (W, Lesson 338).

Let's consider some common colloquial expressions that indicate that someone or something outside you is causing your pain, disease, or loss:

- "You make me sick."
- "You'll be the death of me."
- "My kid is a pain in the neck."
- "My boss is a pain in the butt."
- "My ex-wife is a ballbuster."
- "This project is a real headache."
- "I can't stomach that co-worker."
- "My boyfriend broke my heart."
- "My mother's demands are suffocating me."
- "My kid's college education cost me an arm and a leg."
- "The other team kicked our ass."
- "The economy is crippling me."
- "I'm sweating out this exam."
- "That movie is a real tearjerker."
- "I'm tired of your lies."
- "My statistics professor puts me to sleep."
- "She'll talk you deaf, dumb, and blind."
- "Getting laid off was a real slap in the face."

- "The way he looks at me makes my skin crawl."
- "I'm itching to get out of this house."
- "Betraying my confidence was a stab in the back."
- "What do you want—blood?!"

While we might not think too hard about these expressions when we utter them, or argue that they are just "figures of speech," they demonstrate how we use our bodily experience to play out the guilt and blame we project onto others and ourselves.

In the brilliant parable *Jonathan Livingston Seagull*, author Richard Bach states that *your body is your thoughts in a form you can see*. A healthy body mirrors thoughts of wellness. A sick body "outpictures" thoughts of illness. If you believe others can hurt you, or you perceive value in touting your wounds, your broken body will tell that story. By contrast, if you understand that your happiness is independent of the actions of others, your body will express vitality.

Your body speaks in physical condition what your mouth is not saying with words. My friend Carl was unhappily living with a woman on the East Coast. He wanted to get out of the relationship, but he kept putting off making the break. At the completion of a business trip to California, Carl's friend was driving him to the airport to return home. Suddenly Carl had pains in his chest and he felt faint, to the point that his friend had to stop the car to let Carl get out and lie down on a grassy area beside the road. His body was speaking the unspoken statement, "I don't want to go back there. Too much heartache." That episode got Carl's attention, and he ended the relationship.

Through bodily expression we give ourselves the messages we need to hear, and we communicate to others the messages we want them to hear. If instead we communicate directly and take the actions prompted by our inner guidance, we won't need the body to express the words or actions our soul is calling us to speak and do.

## Who's the Matter with You?

Now we're ready for an inquiry that will begin to undo your suffering:

Describe a pain, ailment, or illness you have now or have had, and then describe who or what is responsible for causing you that trouble.

Examples:

- *Backache:* I have to work terribly hard to support my family.

- *Headache:* The kids were nuts today.

- *Arthritis:* My husband is keeping me in a box. I can't move.

- *Urinary issues:* My partner pisses me off.

- *Ulcer:* Competition in my field could put me out of business if I don't hustle.

Your turn:

| Illness, pain, or loss | Person or situation responsible |
|---|---|
| | |
| | |
| | |
| | |
| | |

In all these cases, someone or something "out there" has cast your trouble upon you, and your ailment is the cross you bear as a consequence. The source of your difficulty might be a person, company, institution, economy, bacteria, religious faction, political party, government, or stellar alignment. Or the demon might be a more nebulous entity, such as neighbors in general, time, humanity, the world, or God. Yet the dynamic is always the same: Someone outside you, more powerful than you, has caused you to lose. ACIM tells us that even the slightest sigh is an expression of a belief in victimhood (W-167.2:6).

## The Way Out

If you've stayed with me this far, you are ready for the way out:

First, recognize that no person, group, situation, or condition has the power to take away your happiness. *No one. No thing. Never.* The experience of joy is your God-given right, a sovereign domain you alone command. "I have a kingdom I must rule" (W-236.1:1). People can *try* to remove your happiness. They can threaten you; criticize you; insult you; tell lies about you; try to frighten, intimidate, or punish you; and do bad things to your body. But they cannot remove your peace unless you give them that power. Your wellness is God's factory-installed gift to you, your inalienable birthright. If anyone *seems* to have stolen your peace, it is because you have allowed them into your sacred sanctuary and let them plunder your treasure. ". . . it does not seem I am [my kingdom's] king at all. It seems to triumph over me, and tell me what to think, and what to do and feel" (W-236.1:2–3).

Yet:

> For you was peace created, given you by its Creator, and established as His Own eternal gift. How can you fail, when you but ask for what He wills for you?
>
> — W-185.12:1-2

We have all heard stories of people who have kept their light shining in the direst circumstances—in concentration camps; in the aftermath of atomic bombing; during natural disasters; and in the midst of economic depressions, famines, and wars. While others were fearful and suffering, certain individuals tapped into faith that transcended appearances. "I could see peace instead of this" (W, Lesson 34).

I saw an interview with a Tibetan Buddhist monk who had been imprisoned by the Chinese for many years. The interviewer asked him, "Were you ever in any real danger?"

"Yes," the monk answered. "Several times."

"Were those the times you were tortured?"

"No, those were the moments when I became angry."

The monk defined danger not as the loss of physical freedom. He defined danger as the loss of spiritual peace.

You and I may not be ready to hold the light in a concentration camp or in the aftermath of an atomic explosion, but Thanksgiving dinner with your family would be a good place to start. If a certain relative bugs you, consider that his behavior is not an attack. It is simply data—something that someone does. Uncle Morty's abrasive jokes are a sign that the poor guy must be in a great deal of pain. His sarcastic barbs are his way of projecting his sins onto the goat (that would be you) and trying to drive it out of the camp. But he cannot accomplish that unless you agree that you are a goat and you are willing to spend your life in the desert. His unkind words are a veiled call for love. His jokes cannot hurt you unless you imbue them with the power to hurt. You are unassailable, connected to the Source of Life no matter what Uncle Morty says or does. If you can come to the awareness that "in my defenselessness my safety lies," you have graduated from the Uncle Morty School of Awakening. Either he will go away or he will no longer be able to ruin your Thanksgiving. In either case you are free.

My sinlessness protects me from all harm.

— W, Lesson 337

## From Death to Life

The second step to reverse pain or illness is to replace the projection of sin with the extension of love. Spin the situation in your favor. You have spun it *against* yourself; now spin it *for* yourself. Your new statement is "Behold me, brother, at your hand I *live*."

Instead of blaming people you believe have hurt you, give them credit for helping you. They are not devils, but angels.

There are two ways to turn devils into angels: First, acknowledge things about them that you genuinely appreciate. Uncle Morty took you to the beach when you were a kid. Your mom still sends you money on your birthday. Your ex-wife is a good mother to your children. There must be *something* you sincerely appreciate about this person. Shift your attention from the mean and nasty things they have said or done to the kind and helpful things they have said or done—even if there are just a few or even only one. You have defined this person by their iniquities. You can just as easily—actually, *more* easily—define them by their redeeming qualities. It's your movie. Change the script.

Perhaps you are still arguing that the person who has hurt you has no redeeming qualities whatsoever. She is evil incarnate, Rosemary's baby conceived with Satan himself, poster child for the dark side of the Force, destined to wreak havoc and horror in the lives of everyone she touches. A nastier bitch never walked the earth.

Got it.

Let's say all of this is true—the person who troubles you is a no-good, cheating, lying SOB. Now here's the second devil-transformer. Consider: How has this person helped you to grow? What spiritual muscles have you developed that you would not have built if this person had been nicer to you? Have you learned to hold your power and self-esteem in the presence of attempted insult? Do you now speak your truth more quickly and directly? Are you now asking for what you want instead of passively deferring? Are you setting healthier boundaries? Have you deepened in patience and compassion? Do you make more self-honoring choices? There are many benefits you might have gained, or still might gain, from someone who challenges you. Consider the man in ancient Greece who paid a fellow the equivalent of a hundred dollars a day to follow him around and insult him, so the recipient could grow beyond insult. (It is said, "An insult is a boon to a sage.") So you can be grateful that your personal Cruella De Vil hasn't sent you an invoice for services rendered!

Everyone helps us. Some help us by being kind, and some help us by acting unkind, so that we may choose kindness no matter what they do. You have a soul contract with your adversary to help you advance spiritually. He is your dear friend who has agreed to wear the costume of enemy to motivate you to reclaim your power. The most brilliant actors take the parts of the creepiest characters. After the play, when they have removed their costumes, they are often quite nice people, entirely unlike the persona they donned for the performance. Pay less attention to their act onstage, and sit with them in the dressing room after the show, sipping a glass of wine together and laughing about the night's performance. Recognize their true friendship and support, expressed through their talent to play a convincing bad guy.

You will never gain by blaming others for your loss. You will always gain by honoring others for their contribution. This reversal of perspective is the most helpful shift in perception you will ever achieve.

## *The Wisdom of Gratitude*

Truly successful people never balk, "At your hand I die." Instead, they credit other people for their success, in essence saying, "At your hand I live." Metaphysically speaking, others are not responsible for your success. You are successful because you choose to be. Yet thanking other people for their gifts to you makes for a more fun and productive journey than blaming them for their misdeeds.

Great managers, leaders, sports heroes, and award winners attribute their accomplishments to their friends, colleagues, teammates, family, staff, and God. World Series winners talk about what a great team they are honored to play with. Academy Award recipients read long lists of names of those who have empowered them to shine. People who have been healed thank God. Business leaders send notes of gratitude to co-workers who put their project over the top. Wise politicians honor their constituents. When President Barack Obama was elected to his second term, he sent out a simple tweet to millions of followers: "This happened because of you. Thank you."

You don't need to be or stay sick, poor, dumped, lonely, or hurt. These conditions are the result of interpretations you lay over events. When you accept 100 percent of the responsibility for the choices you have made, you gain 100 percent of the power to make new and better choices. You can point the power of your thoughts in a new direction and bring healing and life where you once saw illness and death. To utter "At your hand I live" is to tear the mask off the devil and behold instead the Son of God.

> Nothing external to your mind can hurt or injure you in any way. There is no cause beyond yourself that can reach down and bring oppression. No one but yourself affects you. There is nothing in the world that has the power to make you ill or sad, or weak or frail. But it is you who have the power to dominate all things you see by merely recognizing what you are.
>
> — W-190.5:2-6

## Who Is the Author of *A Course in Miracles*?

The author of *A Course in Miracles* identifies himself as Jesus Christ. The voice that dictated the Course makes many references to events in the life of Christ as recorded in the New Testament, including the crucifixion and resurrection, describing the experiences as his own. The author also refers to many statements attributed to Christ in the New Testament as his own. Beyond the verbiage, the wisdom, compassion, and vision imbued in ACIM clearly represent the man who walked the earth as Jesus.

Yet the Jesus who speaks in the Course takes the teachings of Christ to a deeper, richer, and more profound level than is generally understood by readers of the New Testament and many Christians. The author cites biblical phrases and concepts that have been distorted by fear and guilt, and he reinterprets them in the light of innocence, forgiveness, and our unbreakable unity with God. Thus Jesus as author of the Course is not the figure most people know— not because the two are different, but because we often regard the biblical Jesus through a sullied lens. The Jesus behind *A Course in Miracles* represents love and only love.

Dr. Helen Schucman, who meticulously recorded the wisdom she received, never claimed that she was the author of the Course. She assumed the role of a scribe and would have remained anonymous if her peers had not introduced her to readers. Before her death, Dr. Schucman gave strict instructions to her family that at her funeral there was to be no mention of her as the scribe of *A Course in Miracles.* She remained humble about her role, cosmically significant though it was, from the moment the voice first spoke to her to the end of her earthly journey.

Whether or not you believe that Jesus Christ is the author of *A Course in Miracles* is less important than that you receive and live its teachings. Like all spiritual instruction, the value of the material is that it improves the quality of your life, regardless of who spawned it. Focus on the message rather than the messenger. Any arguments over the authorship of *A Course in Miracles* are a waste of precious time. The Course states that it is not interested in controversy, a delaying tactic of the ego. The Course is interested only in healing.

If believing that Jesus Christ is the author of ACIM brings you solace, let your intuition and faith guide you. If you are unsure as to whether or not Jesus gave us the Course, hold that question in abeyance while the material blesses you. All that matters is the awakening of your soul. All else is detail.

# 7

# ISN'T THAT SPECIAL?

My client Stephanie is a successful 38-year-old CPA at a prestigious corporation. She is divorced with a preteen son and daughter. Stephanie is smart, healthy, attractive, and respected among her peers. She earns a substantial income and owns a lovely house in an upscale community. Yet for all of her success, Stephanie carries a quiet heartache. She is missing her life partner. Everything in her life clicks except for a meaningful relationship with that special someone.

Stephanie has told me horror stories about the men she has dated. Some were needy; many just wanted sex; others were narcissistic; one was a rageaholic; and a few, she found out, were married. One guy got drunk at a professional meeting and embarrassed her in front of her colleagues. Several proposed, but none she could imagine being with for a lifetime. "The guys I want don't want me. The guys who want me, I don't want . . . Will I ever find my mate?"

Stephanie's situation is all too familiar. Why have so many of us borne so much pain and disappointment in relationships? Why is it so hard to find someone who matches our values and visions? Why do partnerships that began with passion deteriorate to become stale, boring, or bitter? Why do so many people search for fulfillment outside their primary relationship? Why do we fight with people we once cared about deeply? Why is the divorce rate so high? Why do so many people go from relationship to relationship, marriage to marriage, and still feel empty and alone?

*A Course in Miracles* sheds welcome light on this painful dynamic, along with its remedy. The Course devotes a great deal of ink to *special relationships*. While we all want to meet and bask in the presence of that special someone, the Course uses the word *special* in a unique way.

In a special relationship we single out a person, object, or ideology to be the source of our happiness. We believe we are empty, alone, needy, or defective, or our life is dull, meaningless, painful, or filled with drama. Then we bestow a person or external object with the power to save us from our sense of lack and make us happy. The idea that "you complete me" is the definitive maxim of the special relationship. The belief that someone else can complete you implies that you are incomplete. This erroneous self-image is the root cause of all emotional pain because it is untrue. You are not incomplete, and no one can complete you. You are eternally, unassailably, undeniably whole.

The fatal flaw in the "you complete me" formula is that if someone has the power to complete you by doing what makes you happy, he or she has the power to render you once again incomplete by withdrawing the behavior that validates you. While being with your "completer" feels heady and exhilarating, if the relationship tanks, you crash to the depths of despair and you feel lonelier than ever. If receiving a phone call from him sends you to heaven, waiting by the phone when he doesn't call sends you to hell. If you are "in love" with the way she looks, when her looks change, you will fall out of "love." If his declaration that you make his life worth living makes you feel secure, the day he chooses to go fishing with his buddies rather than be with you leaves you feeling worthless.

Special love is a drug, and an addictive one at that. The more you indulge it, the more you need it. When it goes away, you plunge into severe withdrawal.

> For an unholy relationship is based on differences, where each one thinks the other has what he has not. They come together, each to complete himself and rob the other. They stay until they think that there is nothing left to steal, and then move on. And so they wander through a world of strangers, unlike themselves, living with their bodies

perhaps under a common roof that shelters neither; in the same room and yet a world apart.

— T-22.In.2:5-8

Then, as the pattern goes, you seek and find another person or object to fill the role of savior. "Another can be found" (W-170.8:7). The ego provides an endless list of special objects. But this is not the answer to your emptiness, no more than another injection of heroin is the answer to the addict's craving. "All things you seek to make your value greater in your sight limit you further, hide your worth from you, and add another bar across the door that leads to true awareness of your Self" (W-128.3:3). Sooner or later your next special relationship will wobble and dissolve, and you are back where you started, or even worse off.

You cannot isolate something outside yourself as the source of your good or sorrow and remain at peace with yourself. When you make something special, you give it unique power to save or damn. No thing has such power or deserves it. Only *you* have that power, and when you withdraw it from your designated object, you find healing and redemption that no person or thing can or will ever bring you. The special someone you have been looking for is *you*. "My salvation comes from me" (W, Lesson 70).

## Many Forms of Specialness

We form special relationships not just with romantic partners, but with friends, companies, possessions, and ideologies. You can weave an aura of specialness around a teacher, therapist, guru, pet, sport, diet, house, article of clothing, or car. You might go gaga over a movie star, rock icon, or author. You can get attached to an ideology, such as that of a political party. Radio and television broadcasts are replete with red-faced commentators shouting about why their party is always right and the other party is always wrong. You can get stuck on a place, such as needing to get your desired room at the hotel where you vacation every summer. And the list goes on. The ego can use *any* object as a target for special-ness, and, given the freedom to do so, it will.

My mentor was a yoga master who hiked high into the Hima-layas to a remote ashram reputed for its tranquil meditative at-mosphere. As she approached the temple she heard a voice shout, "That's my pillow!" Immediately another voice retorted, "No, it's *my* pillow!"

Two yogis were fighting over a certain meditation pillow, which they each believed would help them find deeper peace. On and on they bickered. These two ascetics had renounced ev-erything else in the world, but they still believed they needed a special pillow. In believing the pillow could take them to heaven, they each went to hell—for that moment, at least.

Many of us have a special relationship with money. If we have it we feel secure, and if we lack it we feel limited. Money provides a classic example of giving your power to an external symbol. People fight over money, kill for it, and ruin loving friendships. Countless crimes have been committed for "the almighty dollar." Countries wage economic-based wars that destroy human beings by the millions. The painful quest for specialness affects not just individuals, but nations and cultures.

Ironically, religion is one of the most often used vehicles for special relationships. Many people believe that their religion is closer to God than anyone else's. Adherents driven by "faith" have fought long, bloody wars, and countless people have been mur-dered in the name of a special religion. Yet God has no part in the killing. It is but specialness that destroys. In the documentary movie *Oh My God,* we meet a Christian owner of a gun shop in Texas. "Everyone who does not believe in Jesus Christ is going to hell," she swears. Then in the Middle East we find a devout Muslim who declares, "Everyone who does not worship Allah is going to hell," and on and on. Religious specialness separates people from each other and God, under the illusion of drawing them closer.

You can form a special relationship with an event. I met a woman who had written a hit song 30 years earlier. She went on and on about her success with this song. After a while I began to wonder if anything else had happened to her in the last three decades. She seemed so fixated on that one success that nothing since then was worth talking about. I'm sure there were many more riches in and around her that I would have liked to have known about. Yet her true self was buried beneath that one moment of glory, the gold record her headstone.

We all have a special relationship with something. *A Course in Miracles* helps us understand and transform such relationships using the tools I will soon explain.

## Special Hate Behind Special Love

Special love relationships are fueled by special hate. When you turn the power of your happiness over to someone, you hate them for being able to pull your strings. Why would you like—let alone love—someone who can make you miserable? So behind the soft whispers and rocking sex, anger simmers and erupts when you get rubbed the wrong way.

Simultaneously you hate yourself for selling out. To indulge in special love, you must see yourself as deficient, empty, and incapable of fulfilling your own happiness. That's a terrible way to regard yourself. You demean yourself by needing someone else to validate you.

This is why special love relationships turn so quickly to special hate. Scratch the surface with an unkind word, wanton glance, or missed anniversary, and the "love" you professed quickly evaporates. If your love for that person was so real and deep, why would an imagined slight turn you against her so quickly and wrathfully? Why do you have the biggest blowups with the people you supposedly love the most? Because the love you profess is not real love. It is special love. Your hidden intention is to get something from that person, something you believe you cannot give yourself. As long as he delivers the goods, you "love" him. But the moment he slips, watch out! The Good Witch of the North quickly morphs to the Wicked Witch of the West.

Special hate behind special love shows up in idolatrous relationships in which you worship a celebrity, teacher, or guru. The word "fan" is a shortened form of the word "fanatic." When you give your power to someone whom you *assume* is closer to beauty, talent, power, success, wealth, wisdom, or God than you are, you have a special relationship with that person. Like the special romantic relationship, your "love" is a thin veil for hating that person for having more than you and controlling your happiness. The rock star Selena was murdered by the former president of her fan club, just as John Lennon was shot by a disgruntled fan. Lots of people have killed (or wish they could kill) their spouses. I read about a woman who hired a hit man to do away with her husband. When the attempt failed and she was arrested, she explained that she put out the contract because her religion didn't allow divorce. O humanity, where lies true love?

One of the clearest illustrations of special hate behind special love comes from the demise of the English explorer Captain James Cook. When Cook and his crew initially landed at Kealakekua Bay on the island of Hawaii, the natives, who had never seen light-skinned people or a clipper ship, believed he and his crew were gods. They worshipped the "gods" and gave them amenities reserved for deities. The ship's crew was happy to take full advantage of the offerings. When one of the "gods" died, and another stole a rowboat belonging to the natives, the Hawaiians realized that the visitors were not gods at all. In a spontaneous riot, a mob overwhelmed and killed Captain Cook and many of his crew. The special "love" by which the Hawaiians had betrayed themselves, bestowing unmerited power on an external source, quickly turned to special hate. As musician Dan McKinnon put it, "It takes only a short fall for a halo to become a noose."

## Healing Special Love

The answer to special relationships, *A Course in Miracles* explains, is a *holy relationship.* In a holy relationship, you do not see yourself as lacking, and you do not bestow your partner with the power to save or damn. You regard both of you as whole, together to discover, magnify, and celebrate the gifts you bring to each other and the world. You recognize that your source of happiness resides *inside* you, and you can choose to feel good regardless of your partner's behavior. Your partner is not the screen onto which you project your unmet needs and upsets, but instead a cherished companion whom you enfold with ever-deeper appreciation. Your purpose together is not to offset each other's deficiencies, but to honor and express your already-existing sufficiency. You do not use the relationship to berate each other, bring one another down, or stuff both of you into suffocating boxes. Instead it is a vehicle to bring forth the best in both of you and fan your light so it shines as brightly as possible.

In the holy relationship, you seek to potentiate each other's joy rather than wrest well-being from your one and only supplier. God is your supply, and your sustenance can come through many avenues, including but not limited to your partner. The love you share runs far deeper than romance, sexual chemistry, personality preferences, or a political alliance. You are not simply two people coming together to offset each other's emptiness. You are God discovering yourself through your beloved.

> A holy relationship starts from a different premise. Each one has looked within and seen no lack. Accepting his completion, he would extend it by joining with another, whole as himself. He sees no difference between these selves, for differences are only of the body. Therefore, he looks on nothing he would take . . . Just under Heaven does he stand . . . For this relationship has Heaven's Holiness. How far from home can a relationship so like to Heaven be?
>
> — T-22.In.3:1-9

## Growing Beyond Form

One way you can cultivate a holy relationship is to release your insistence on the form you believe your partner's behavior should take, and support him on the path of his choice rather than the one you expect. At the same time, stand free of your partner's ego-based demands and expectations. This can be difficult for couples who have been committed to a particular religion, family tradition, business, lifestyle, or routine. If one partner seeks to explore a different path, the other partner may become distressed and put pressure on the spouse to keep coloring within the prescribed lines. The demand that a partner stick with a certain form is a sure sign of a special relationship. Non-attachment to a form is a sign of a healthy, holy relationship.

My coaching client Jodi has been in a Mormon marriage for nearly 30 years. For all those years she, her husband, and their five children have participated avidly in the Church of Jesus Christ of Latter-Day Saints rituals and community.

A few years ago Jodi felt inspired to explore other philosophies, including alternative forms of spiritual expression—all no-no's according to traditional Mormonism, which shuns people who step out of line. So for Jodi to express her desire to delve into nontraditional pathways required a huge leap of faith.

Although Jodi's husband, Don, was initially distressed by her dabbling outside the church, he supported her to venture onto other paths of spiritual inquiry. Jodi took a life coach training, read books by Paramahansa Yogananda, set up an altar that included small statues of Buddha and the Hindu deity Ganesha, and took an unprecedented trip by herself to a residential meditation retreat. If Don had been stuck on their special relationship, he might have hit the ceiling and called in the church fathers to "deprogram" his wife. But, to his credit, he just kept loving Jodi, which endeared him to her all the more. His trust in her explorations did not dissolve their marriage, but strengthened it. When I last spoke to Jodi, she reported that she and Don were doing tantric sex practices. Both of them deserve huge credit for flowing with the changes in their relationship and co-creating a marriage based on love, not fear.

My mother taught me a life-changing lesson in holy family relationships. When I set out on my spiritual path, I was inspired by the teachings of Jesus. I studied the New Testament, and I taped a small picture of Jesus on the dashboard of my car.

My Jewish mother was not exactly pleased as punch to ride with Jesus as a copilot. When I picked her up to take her shopping, she made fun of the picture. "Were you cold out here last night, Jesus?" she mockingly asked the image, tapping it with her forefinger. "Would you like me to knit you a sweater?"

So out of respect for my mother (especially since she had paid for the car), I removed the photo from the dashboard and placed it in the glove box. The next time my mother sat in the car, she said nothing but she seemed happier, so I figured Jesus was secretly smiling under the dashboard.

A few weeks later when I went to visit my mother at her house, I saw something I had never seen before in my home or in any Jewish home. On the dining-room table, propped up against a napkin holder, was a small picture of the Catholic saint Veronica.

Astonished, I asked, "Mom, where did you get this?"

"I saw it at a garage sale," she answered nonchalantly. "I thought you would like it."

I was speechless. In order for my mother to get me that picture, she had to rise above her lifetime belief system and values as a Jew and a Jewish mother.

That was the greatest lesson in unconditional love I have ever learned. At the time, I was teaching yoga and meditation and telling people about unconditional love. Gazing at the picture on my mother's dining-room table, I realized that all of my words were empty. In that one act, my mother demonstrated true love—not the kind you talk about, the kind you live. In that moment she and I entered into the holiest of relationships.

## Can't Smile Without You

The other side of the coin of special love and hate relationships is to be the object of someone projecting special love or hate onto you. Someone may have a crush on you, adore you as a teacher, idolize you as a hero, worship you as a savior, or decide you can fulfill him or her in a way that no one else can.

*Watch out.*

The road of special love always conceals the land mine of special hate. While your ego may be thrilled to bask in someone else's adoration, you will pay a price that far exceeds the glory of your 15 minutes of fame. At some point your admirer will grow disgruntled, find things wrong with you, accuse you of selfish acts, and try to crucify you.

I speak from experience. In my early days as an author, I received numerous letters, many of which crossed the line of appreciation and forged into dysfunctional adoration. Inexperienced in the dynamics of special love, I savored and cultivated communication with these people. Eventually all of those people sent me angry letters accusing me of not being who I said I was. But I never said I was the person they were angry at. They made up a story about who I was, and when I did not live up to their story, the shift hit the fan. Now I don't indulge anyone who sees me with stars in their eyes. To the contrary, I keep them at a distance. I am not their answer. I am a person, just like them, on my path to greater clarity. Plato said, "True friendship can occur only among equals."

You might also be the target of someone who decides to bypass special love and go directly for special hate. Someone who is wounded or emotionally unstable might make you the object of their angry campaign. In such a case, the vendetta is not about you. It is about that person's projection onto you. If you defend yourself or retaliate, you will just dig deeper into the mire. ("Never wrestle with a pig," goes an idiom attributed to George Bernard Shaw. "You'll both get dirty and the pig likes it.") Instead, regard the person's attack as a call for love. Simply trust in the reality of well-being and stand firm in your innocence. "I am in need of nothing but the truth" (W, Lesson 251).

## Tools for Transformation

Special love relationships are the ego's favorite weapon to keep you from peace (see T-16.V.2:3). You believe they will bring you to heaven, but instead they take you to hell. Holy relationships take us to heaven. Distress in a relationship is a sign that specialness has intruded on love. Such a moment offers you a golden opportunity to heal your mind and heart by making a new choice.

> Trials are but lessons that you failed to learn presented once again, so where you made a faulty choice before you now can make a better one, and thus escape all pain that what you chose before has brought to you. In every difficulty, all distress, and each perplexity Christ calls to you and gently says, "My brother, choose again." He would not leave one source of pain unhealed, nor any image left to veil the truth. He would remove all misery from you whom God created altar unto joy. He would not leave you comfortless, alone in dreams of hell, but would release your mind from everything that hides His face from you.
>
> — T-31.VIII.3:1-5

Here are some specific tips on how to transform special relationships into holy ones:

**1. Recognize how much the special love or special hate relationship is costing you.**
Special relationships cost you dearly. They bring you enormous emotional pain, often accompanied by physical distress and significant financial outlay. You cannot afford such suffering. If your relationship is bringing you more sorrow than joy and your losses outweigh your gains, you must not continue as you have been. Tell the truth about what in your relationship is working and what is not, what hurts and what heals. Denial of your pain will not serve you. Honesty will. Authentic communication is the first step to transforming special relationships into holy relationships.

### 2. Shift your vision.

If you are in pain with a partner or any object of specialness, you are not seeing that person or object clearly. You are seeing *your version* of that person or object. If you were to see your partner as he or she is, you would experience only love and appreciation. But the veils of illusion distort our perception so we see only selected fragments of the whole. Anger is a sign that you are focusing on limiting or illusory aspects to justify your judgments. "I am upset because I see something that is not there" (W, Lesson 6). To heal your relationship, seek, find, and focus on aspects that support a version of the partner you prefer. Quit harping on his or her faults, reward desirable traits, and potentiate the behaviors and relationship you desire. Dale Carnegie advised, "Give the other person a fine reputation to live up to."

I had a neighbor I regarded as a nasty alcoholic. Brenda would sit at the kitchen table with her husband, drink, and complain. I did not see any good in her. Then she and her husband took in a younger fellow to live with them. Mark helped the couple around the house and stayed with them for years. When Brenda passed away, Mark told me, "Brenda was one of the kindest people I have ever known. She and her husband treated me like a son. I will always remember and love her." In that moment, I realized how skewed was my interpretation of Brenda. I was focusing on one aspect of her that brought me pain to consider. Mark, on the other hand, focused on an aspect of Brenda that brought him joy. Each of us was reaping the result of our interpretation. From that moment on, I began to think of Brenda as a kind person, which has brought me peace.

You cannot control the behavior of others, and you cannot dictate the choices they make. But you have total control over which aspects of them you are selecting to magnify in your experience. This is where your true authority lives. "My Father gives all power unto me" (W, Lesson 320).

Practicing the principle of *Experience follows vision* will transform your relationship with an object such as money. If financial interactions are stressful for you, you are not seeing money clearly. You are seeing your negative interpretation of money.

Money is a neutral thing, and there is nothing inherently stressful about it. Stress is far more attitudinal than situational. The idea that "money is the root of all evil" is fabricated by the ego, which is infatuated with evil and its causes. The Spiritual Eye, by contrast, sees money as a vehicle to express love. Money blesses you when you receive it, and it blesses you and the recipient when you give it. It is life-giving. *Fear*, not money, is the root of all evil. When you see money as the root of all good, it becomes your friend, finds its way to you, and increases happiness in the world as it circulates to and from you.

### 3. Establish your awareness in the now.

ACIM calls the present moment "the holy instant." Relationship arguments drag the past into the present as artillery to justify your position. It's always about what he or she did rather than who he or she is now. What would you have to argue about if you did not call in the troops of days gone by? You might actually enjoy the now moment, fresh and clean, with your partner at your side rather than on the opposite side of a battlefield.

### 4. Seek to join rather than separate.

The scribes of *A Course in Miracles* attribute the birth of the Course to their decision to support each other rather than maintain their ongoing conflict. When you do the same, you pave the way for miracles and you heal painful relationships. In the movie *Oh My God,* there is a touching scene in which a Jewish rabbi and a Muslim imam are walking side by side on a street in Jerusalem, arms around each other's waists. This scene was a breath of fresh air after many interviews with hard-core religionists who used their faith as a tool for divisiveness rather than inclusion. When we can all get to the place the rabbi and imam got to, the world will be far closer to heaven.

My client Max was married to Sonia for many years, during which they parented two children. Then Max claimed his gay identity and left his wife for a man, Trevor. Although Sonia was initially shocked and upset by her husband's revelation, she and Max have maintained a loving, supportive relationship. When

Trevor was ill, Sonia went to his home and made him smoothies. Although the way her marriage with Max turned out was certainly not what she expected, Sonia decided that a holy relationship with Max was more important than a special relationship, and that is what they have created. Max still loves and honors Sonia, and speaks of her only in superlatives. The couple would rather give their children a model of kindness than strife, and everyone has benefited as a result.

ACIM tells us that holy relationships, like all miracles, reverse the laws of the world (T-1.I.9:2). Much of the world, especially some religions, would prescribe that a man who leaves his wife for a man should be punished. The laws of God prescribe that he should be loved. The real world as God created it is the opposite of the world the ego has manufactured. Max and Sonia's relationship is a shining example of genuine love. While they are no longer together physically, they are deeply joined spiritually. Holy relationships are the home of miracles.

### 5. Invite Higher Power into your relationship.

If you are having relationship difficulties, it is because you have placed your ego in charge of a domain it is not capable of managing. The ego, which thrives on specialness, does not have the skills to create and maintain a holy relationship. "You cannot be your guide to miracles, for it is you who made them necessary" (T-14.XI.7:1). You cannot get yourself out of a relationship mess with the same mind-set that got you into it. This is where you need the Holy Spirit to help you. The Holy Spirit, as the Course explains, is the part of your mind united with divine wisdom. It is bigger, smarter, clearer, and stronger than any difficulty the ego can conjure or any of the ego's attempted solutions. The Holy Spirit will resolve your relationship issues in miraculous ways. But you must be open to receive its guidance. You must be willing to invite Higher Power to do for you what you have been unable to do for yourself. ". . . the means on which you can depend for miracles has been provided for you. God's Son can make no needs his Father will not meet, if he but turn to Him ever so little" (T-14.XI.7:2–3).

The answer to your relationship challenges is far easier than you have believed. You do not have to do it all yourself. Pray for help with a sincere heart, and you will receive it. You will be told precisely what to do, when, and how. No matter what has happened or is happening with your human partner, you have a Divine Partner who will guide you at every turn and make your relationships on Earth like those in heaven.

## Specialness That Works

*A Course in Miracles* does not ask us to give up special relationships. Attractions and preferences come with the human package. So marry the person who ignites your spirit, hang your hat where you feel at home, worship at the church that expresses your faith, root for your favorite sports team, vacation at your chosen resort, and order crème brûlée for dessert. Just keep your preferences in perspective and don't lose your peace over them. The moment you grow irritable because your spouse doesn't take out the garbage, your flight is delayed, or your neighbors go to the wrong church, specialness has become your captor. If you can get past strangling your partner, throwing tantrums, or burning nonbelievers at the stake, you'll do just fine.

ACIM also acknowledges that you have a special function (T-25.VI). There is a unique path for you, based on your talents, visions, desires, and inclinations. This special function is inspired and guided by Higher Power, Who wants you to fulfill it. Do not try to stifle or extinguish your unique joys, passions, and self-expression. They are all a part of the path that leads to your divine destiny. You have a place in the world that will bring healing to you and others when you claim and act on it.

> To each He gives a special function in salvation he alone can fill; a part for only him. Nor is the plan complete until he finds his special function, and fulfills the part assigned to him, to make himself complete within a world where incompletion rules.
>
> — T-25.VI.4:2-3

Special relationships, challenging as they can be, provide the most fertile ground for transformation. When you turn a special relationship into a holy relationship, you have done the work of a lifetime. "The holiest of all the spots on earth is where an ancient hatred has become a present love" (T-26.IX.6:1). Special human relationships are *already* holy in that you are both gleaming facets of a perfect God, together to discover your magnificence. *A Course in Miracles* helps us peel away the veil of specialness from our holy relationships so we can release, as Robert Browning described it, "the imprisoned splendour."

The direct route to healing relationships is found in Lesson 161: "Give me your blessing, holy son of God." All relationships are given as blessings to expand love in your life. If you do not perceive the blessings, it is only because you have been focused on the shortcomings. Ask, pray, and affirm to find the blessing in your relationship. It is there. The joy and healing you experience from transforming a special relationship to a holy one goes far, far beyond the petty rewards the ego seeks to extract. Richard Bach said, "True love stories never have endings." All relationships are potentially true love stories. When you recognize the gifts they bring, you will thank everyone who has walked by your side, for a moment or a lifetime, and all of your relationships will bless you forever.

> It is no dream to love your brother as yourself . . . Let Him fulfill the function that He gave to your relationship . . . and nothing will be wanting . . .
>
> — T-18.V.5:1,6

# 8

# THE PICTURE
# AND THE FRAME

Vincent van Gogh is one of the most highly valued artists in history. One of his paintings sold in 1990 for $82.5 million ($149 million today, adjusted for inflation), and all of his paintings are valued at $700 million in current dollars. During his lifetime van Gogh sold but one painting, for 400 francs. His paintings were considered so worthless that they were sold in bunches—not for the artwork, but for their wooden frames. Buyers thought they would make good kindling for fires. Van Gogh deemed himself a failure and committed suicide.

In "The Two Pictures" (T-17.IV), *A Course in Miracles* uses the analogy of a picture and a frame as a key teaching metaphor for how to heal our special relationships. One picture is set within a huge gaudy frame that grabs all of our attention, to the point that we hardly notice the picture. The other picture is set in a much more modest and tasteful frame that highlights the splendor of the picture.

> The special relationship has the most imposing and deceptive frame of all the defenses the ego uses. Its thought system is offered here, surrounded by a frame so heavy and so elaborate that the picture is almost obliterated by its imposing structure. Into the frame are woven all sorts of fanciful and fragmented illusions of love, set with dreams of sacrifice and self-aggrandizement, and interlaced with gilded threads of self-destruction. The glitter of blood shines like rubies, and the tears are faceted like diamonds and gleam in the dim light in which the offering is made.

> Look at the *picture.* Do not let the frame distract you . . .
> The frame is not the gift.
>
> — EXCERPTED FROM T-17.IV.8-9

The Course uses such dramatic imagery here because it needs to get our attention, to dislodge us from the ego's most cherished illusion. The world is fascinated with frames more than pictures, form more than essence. We are so enthralled with the wrapping that we miss the present. We are enticed by the babe with a hot body; the magnate with big bucks; the job with copious perks; the sprawling house with the portico; the shiny red sports car; the cosmetic surgery that will make us look young and attractive; the recording contract that will rocket us to the top of the charts. These are the glittery toys the ego dangles before us. This is not to say you should not want, have, or enjoy these things. It *is* to say that if you are fascinated with the frame more than the picture, you may gain the world but lose your soul.

The film *Bedazzled* (2000 version) delivers a striking lesson in the contrast between the picture and the frame. Elliot is an un-popular nerd sporting a huge crush on the gorgeous but unattain-able Alison. Enter the devil, who offers Elliot seven chances to be with the girl of his dreams—in exchange for his soul. Elliot agrees. The only problem is that every time Elliot dictates the form by which he will attract Alison, some tragic flaw in his plan sabotages his success. He is wealthy, but she is cheating. He is sensitive, but she is repulsed by his weakness. He is brilliant but gay. Finally Elliot runs out of chances, and the devil is about to take her due. Then he meets an angel in human form who reminds Elliot that his soul belongs to God, and no devil can co-opt it. Reawakened to the value of his spirit, Elliot realizes that what he really wants is a relationship with a real person. Finally the universe engineers a clever way for him to have it—as it will do for you.

I knew a singer who was obsessed with seeing her name in lights in Las Vegas. She was talented, but so focused on becoming a celebrity that she made terrible compromises. She took seedy gigs, slept with creepy producers, and scampered about the globe in a never-ending quest to get lauded and applauded. She finally gave up her quest for fame and had a family, which brought her more fulfillment than the anxiety-ridden world in which she had become embroiled. No career is worth trading for peace.

You might remember the glamorous television special *Who Wants to Marry a Multi-Millionaire?* The show was devoted to wide-eyed maidens parading their wares before an eligible wealthy bachelor. Finally he chose one candidate and they were married on the show. Huge publicity. Astronomical ratings. Names became household words. The marriage lasted just a few weeks. Glitz? Plenty. Substance? None. Big frame? The biggest. Picture? So flimsy that it crumbled at first touch.

Two pictures, two frames. Big frame, little picture. Big picture, little frame. Frames are useful if they magnify the beauty of the subject they highlight. The subject is you. The frame is the world. Keep them in order.

## Really Happy Now

At every moment a treasure is being offered you. But you will receive it only if you are looking in the right place. When you shift your vision from the frame to the picture, you will find the masterpiece. Even if you have overlooked the gifts offered you, they have been kept intact, awaiting your recognition and acceptance. The Course tells us, "My treasure house is full, and angels watch its open doors that not one gift is lost, and only more are added" (W-316.1:4).

> The holy instant is . . . a picture, too, set in a frame. Yet if you accept this gift you will not see the frame at all, because the gift can only be accepted through your willingness to focus all your attention on the picture.
>
> — T-17.IV.11:1-3

Louise Hay took me out to lunch in her gold Rolls-Royce. The vehicle was an ode to itself. When the manufacturer installs the elegant wood trim on the interior of one of their cars, the company keeps the exact tree from which the wood was hewn. So if you ever need your wood trim replaced, the replacement will be an exact match to the original. Part of me was really impressed with such immaculate attention to detail. Another part wondered if the tree might have better served the planet by standing in the forest and letting birds nest in its branches. The last time I saw Louise, she had traded her Rolls for a Smart car.

Tom Shadyac is an A-list Hollywood director who rose to fame on big hits like *Ace Ventura: Pet Detective, The Nutty Professor,* and *Bruce Almighty.* Tom lived in a sprawling multimillion-dollar mansion and enjoyed an opulent celebrity lifestyle. All that changed when he sustained a head injury in a bicycle accident and nearly became disabled. Tom rethought his priorities and decided to focus more on happiness than on stuff. He directed an uplifting documentary, *I Am,* and served as executive producer for a follow-up, *Happy,* celebrating pictures over frames. At the conclusion of *I Am,* we see Tom emerging from his trailer-park home (which he chose over the lavish estate he'd had before) and then bicycling to the studio. Now he's successful *and* happy.

ACIM does not call us to trash the frame. It has a purpose. Just keep the frame in service of the picture. Keep your body strong, healthy, and feeling good—not for its own sake, but for the sake of doing things that uplift and ennoble yourself and those you touch. Enjoy your car, but don't worship it. Let sex be an expression of love and caring. Live in a house that makes you happy but doesn't own you. Stuff exists for your sake, not you for it. Use everything you have in the service of Spirit, and Higher Power will take care of the details.

## The Self-Indulgence of Self-Denial

The other side of the coin of indulging the body and coveting things is *denying* the body and things. Bodies and things are not evil, and we do not need to punish or demean them. Fighting or hating form is a disguised way of worshipping it. When you spend your time depriving your body, you are giving it as much attention as indulging it. People who flagellate themselves, physically or emotionally, are just as absorbed in the frame as people who gorge themselves. In both cases the frame is the object of attention rather than the picture. One frame is filled with sensory indulgence. The other is filled with sensory deprivation. It's still all about the frame.

Buddha trod the path of self-indulgence when he lived as Gautama, a prince in a luxurious castle. Then he renounced his royal riches and became an ascetic, spending years fasting and mortifying his flesh. Finally a woman took pity on Gautama and gave him a bowl of rice. The moment he accepted, he became the enlightened Buddha. He discovered what he called "the middle path." He ceased to focus on the body and became absorbed in the spirit. Waging war on your body only glorifies it. *"Do not fight yourself"* (T-30.I.1:7). Beating yourself up physically or emotionally saps love from the world. Treating yourself gently, gracefully, and respectfully brings more light to humanity. The only question worth asking about any act is, "Does this bring more joy into the world, or does it diminish joy in the world?" Here you have the simplest yet the most effective guide to all life choices.

> Miracles reawaken the awareness that the spirit, not the body, is the altar of truth. This is the recognition that leads to the healing power of the miracle.
>
> — T-1.I.20:1-2

## Lifestyles of the Rich in Spirit

John Robbins was heir to the Baskin-Robbins ice-cream empire. He stood to inherit a fortune and gain financial security for life. At a young age John researched the effect of the dairy industry on the health of human beings and the planet, and decided that milk derivatives are hurting more than helping. He turned his back on his successorship, became a vegan, and wrote a landmark book that was nominated for a Pulitzer Prize: *Diet for a New America.*

One day John and his wife, Deo, received a phone call from the producer of the *Lifestyles of the Rich and Famous* television series, asking if a crew could visit the Robbins' home and interview them. The producer thought it would be a good novelty interview to show the alternative lifestyle the Robbins family had chosen. The crew came to the Robbins' humble home in the hills near Santa Cruz, California, where they received heartfelt hospitality and home-cooked meals. By the end of the day, the crew didn't want to leave. They found the family refreshingly real in contrast to their regular interviewees, whose lives revolved around their homes and possessions. John quipped that perhaps someone should produce a new show: *Lifestyles of the Rich in Spirit.*

One of my clients is the daughter of one of the wealthiest families in America. She doesn't like to go to family gatherings because all her relatives talk about is what they are doing with their money. They run their family like a board of directors. When a few of the family teenagers were caught smoking pot at the estate, the family got together to vote on whether the kids should be allowed to continue. I don't know how the vote turned out. I imagine the kids are still smoking somewhere. You can't legislate higher consciousness. You can only live it.

My friend Raymond is also extraordinarily wealthy. He likes to use money to rebuild companies that are falling apart. He told me, "I channel money." Raymond funded his wife's mail-order business to bring ACIM-related products to the world. Their money is put to good use. Money is the frame, not the picture. And in these cases, what lovely pictures it frames.

## Corporate Heartquarters

The word *corporation* is related to the word *corporeal* and other words deriving from the Latin *corpus,* meaning "body." A corporation is just a big body. If you want to understand the dynamics of a body as it is projected onto a larger screen, observe corporations. Like individuals, corporate bodies can frame a picture of service, or they can become goals unto themselves. Many institutions set out with positive intentions to improve the world, but then they become driven by money, power, and ego, and they drift from the goals for which they were established. Then the frame supplants the picture, narcissism replaces vision, and self-glorification substitutes for bettering the lives of customers. When the institution becomes sterile and hollow, the people who work there hate their jobs, service flatlines, and the company, no longer founded in integrity, cannot continue. Truth nourishes; illusions kill. "Nothing can be apart from Him and live" (W-156.2:9).

My friend Gillian was the minister of a spirit-filled church that grew in popularity and eventually purchased a building that required a huge mortgage. During the building-fund campaign, several donors made substantial contributions and then wished to be on the board of directors. Feeling obligated to these donors, Gillian placed them on the board. Then these managers began to steer the church in directions that compromised its integrity. Severe infighting and power struggles broke out within the board, which spilled over to the congregation. The church that was originally created to bring people closer to heaven became a living hell. At that point Gillian resigned from the church and left it to its own warring devices. It was not long before the church disintegrated, for it was no longer founded on the spirit that conceived it.

The universe is set up to prosper what is sourced by Spirit, and to disintegrate what is ego driven. Egos can drive for a while, but eventually their efforts must falter. Powerful as Hitler seemed for a short time, truth would not sustain evil. If your endeavors are founded in life-sustaining values, they will thrive. If life force is absent, they will die.

Several decades ago a new East Coast–based airline grew at a phenomenal rate. Within a few years the company took over most of the Newark airport and was flying to many cities around the globe. Flight attendants bragged to passengers, "You are now flying on the fastest-growing airline in U.S. history."

A year later the airline was out of business. The company didn't lay a firm foundation for growth and tried to do too much too soon. It was interested in expansion more than service, visibility more than authority. Alignment with universal principles is all the alignment you will ever need.

## What's Really Important

After Steven Jobs was diagnosed with cancer, he delivered a commencement address at Stanford University. "Death is very likely the single best invention of life," he stated.

There is great meaning behind this apparently odd statement. *A Course in Miracles* tells us repeatedly that death is not real. There is only life; death exists only at the surface level of forms and appearances. Death is the universe's way of clearing out what has served its purpose, to make way for the next act of purpose. When the body has completed its mission, it will gently be laid aside (W-294.1:7). Death forces us to confront the mortality of the body and inquire more deeply as to who we truly are and what we are here for. It moves us to ask, "Am I the picture or am I the frame? Am I a body or am I the Spirit?" Many ACIM lessons poignantly answer this question, in particular, "I am not a body. I am free. For I am still as God created me" (W, Lesson 201), and "There is no death. The Son of God is free" (W, Lesson 163).

Just a little earlier in Steve Jobs's Stanford commencement address, he said,

> Remembering that I'll be dead soon is the most important tool I've ever encountered to help me make the big choices in life. Because almost everything—all external expectations, all pride, all fear of embarrassment or failure—these things just fall away in the face of death, leaving only what is truly important. Remembering that you are going to die is the best way I know to avoid the trap of thinking you have something to lose. You are already naked. There is no reason not to follow your heart.

We need not stand at death's door before we contemplate the purpose of our life and activate our spiritual intention. We simply need to remember what's important—the picture, rather than the frame—as we move through our daily activities.

The film *About Time* portrays the journey of a man who has the power to travel back in time and change the events that shaped his destiny. After experimenting with changes he believed would improve his lot, eventually he decides to leave everything just as it is. "Let all things be exactly as they are" (W, Lesson 268). Director Richard Curtis said of his movie, "I thought it would be fascinating to make a film in which the climax of the film is a man's choice to fully live an ordinary day." Such a choice makes every day extraordinary.

> Who hangs an empty frame upon a wall and stands before it, deep in reverence, as if a masterpiece were there to see? Yet if you see your brother as a body, it is but this you do. The masterpiece that God has set within this frame is all there is to see . . . Yet what God has created needs no frame . . . His masterpiece He offers you to see.
>
> — T-25.II.5:1-6

## Is *A Course in Miracles* Christian?

It would certainly appear that *A Course in Miracles* is a Christian text, considering the many references to Christ, the Holy Spirit, the crucifixion, the resurrection, salvation, and redemption. Being written in the voice of Jesus Christ would seem to cinch ACIM as an opus of the Christian religion.

Yet there is far more to *A Course in Miracles* than can be embraced by any one religion, including Christianity. The Course belongs to all religions and to none.

Upon closer inspection, the philosophy of *A Course in Miracles* is in some ways more akin to Advaita Vedanta and Buddhism rather than Christianity as we know it. *Advaita* means "non-dualism," affirming the oneness of life rather than fracturing God into shards, as we do when we look around and observe many forms apparently separated from each other and God. The foremost exponent of Advaita Vedanta in the modern age was the illumined sage Ramana Maharshi, who lived from 1879 to 1950.

The teachings of Sri Ramana are strikingly identical to *A Course in Miracles:*

The real is ever as it is.

All that is required is to cease regarding as real that which is unreal.

The world does not exist in sleep and forms a projection of your mind in the waking state. It is therefore an idea and nothing else.

Your true nature is that of infinite spirit.

— FROM *THE ESSENTIAL TEACHINGS
OF RAMANA MAHARSHI: A VISUAL
JOURNEY,* BY MATTHEW GREENBLATT

The truth is true, no matter who utters it. *A Course in Miracles* embraces the best elements of Christianity, along with themes enunciated by prophets, healers, and sages of all religions, as well as those who teach awakening outside the context of religion.

The Course was birthed in a culture that is predominantly Christian. The author chose to speak in the religious language with which most people are familiar. An ancient Hebrew teaching declares, "The Bible is written in the language of people," meaning that God reaches us in terms we can understand.

Yet there is an even deeper purpose behind the Christian terminology: The Course serves as a correction to what Christianity has become. Although Jesus delivered a pure healing message, the religion that grew up in his name has often been infused with fear, guilt, threats, punishment, and mass murder. Countless atrocities have been committed in the name of Christ, the fear of hell causes innocent souls to tremble, and the injunction to sacrifice has supplanted passion and joy. Jesus dictated *A Course in Miracles* to get Christianity back on track with its true purpose of healing.

The message of ACIM is for all people open to accept and live it, Christians as well as those of other religions or no religion. Many Christians embrace *A Course in Miracles* as an affirmation and deepened expression of their faith. Some Christians reject the Course as the work of the devil. They feel threatened by the Course, since it does not fall within the confines of their belief system. Such a sense of danger and defensiveness is fueled by fear, the experience the Course has come to offset.

*A Course in Miracles* acknowledges and celebrates the God in all people, no matter their faith. Many Christian, Jewish, Muslim, Hindu, and Buddhist practitioners study the Course, as well as people who do not associate with a religion. ACIM is not for everyone, but it is not against anyone. The Course does not call students to evangelize, proselytize, or dislodge anyone from their chosen path. It simply calls us, each and all, to be the light of the world.

# 9

# THE END OF
# SUFFERING

When master healer Patricia Sun gave a lecture in New York City, she explained that the key to personal and planetary healing is to love people and situations we once believed were unlovable. A Jewish woman in the audience challenged her: "I can't love everyone . . . I will never, never, never love Adolf Hitler."

"Let me pose a situation to you," Patricia offered. "Imagine that you personally knew Adolf Hitler when he was a little boy. He was the son of an alcoholic father and a mentally ill mother. The child was subject to terribly dysfunctional influences that set in motion the dynamics for him to perpetrate the heinous acts he ultimately committed. Now imagine you had some time with that little boy, during which you could show him sincere love and soften or offset the dark influence his parents exerted upon him. Imagine that the kindness you gave him nourished his soul in such a way that when he grew up, he would choose a different path and not commit the crimes against humanity that he did. Given that opportunity, would you love that little boy?"

The woman grew silent. Finally she answered, "Certainly."

At the conclusion of the program, a short elderly woman approached Patricia to thank her for the seminar. When the woman reached up to hug her, the sleeve of her dress slipped back to reveal tattooed numbers on her forearm, indicating she had been a prisoner in a Nazi concentration camp. The woman told Patricia, "Every word you said is true."

Those words coming from a Holocaust survivor are far more potent than if they had come from someone with lesser trials. If a woman who had been through such horrors could recognize the power of love to heal, you and I are certainly capable of offering magnanimity of heart when faced with the challenges of our daily lives.

Adolf Hitler did not personally kill millions of people and ravage the world with unprecedented evil and destruction. Sixteen million soldiers collaborated in his dirty work, while more than 50 million other Germans stood by. If you watch film footage of thousands of German soldiers parading before Hitler, their arms shooting into the air as they goose-step, it is obvious that they have been hypnotized by a dark and evil energy. The problem was not one crazed man. The problem was that a nation followed him.

The way to prevent future Hitlers is to not fall prey to the kind of fear, hatred, and mania to which the Germans succumbed. This is why ACIM's assertion that your primary responsibility as a miracle worker is to allow your mind to be healed (T-2.V.5) is so crucial. When you refuse to be a pawn of fear, you reduce the ability of insane illusions to run your life and contaminate the lives of others. When you extract the Hitler from your own consciousness, by overcoming it with love, you subtract a measure of fear from the body of humanity and stop suffering from its rampage.

## Where Ego Trips

*A Course in Miracles* identifies the ego as the source of human suffering. Let's get clear on what the ego is, how it operates, the effects it exerts on your life, and how you can make it work on your behalf rather than allowing it to ravage your happiness.

The ego is a severely limited idea about who and what you are. It defines you as a body only, confined within the boundaries of your flesh, subject to all the laws and experiences that affect bodies. As a body, you are weak and vulnerable amidst a universe filled with threats from sources more powerful than you. Diseases, heart attacks, auto accidents, airplane crashes, demented gunmen, earthquakes, tsunamis, and nuclear war can wipe you from existence in a second. The world is a dangerous place where you must protect and defend yourself at every turn. If necessary, you must attack before you are attacked. If you want to see and hear a litany of all the bad things that can happen to bodies, turn on the evening news.

There was a time when you were not a body or an ego. You were a powerful spiritual being united with God and the entire universe. You knew who you were and enjoyed all the benefits of a divine being. Then a moment came when you ceased to know yourself as a spirit, and you began to regard yourself as a body. That moment occurred in the womb, at the time of your birth, or soon thereafter. You underwent a crucial identity shift. You did not cease to be a spiritual being; you ceased to *know yourself* as a spiritual being. You have seen movies in which the focus of the camera shifts from the actor in the foreground to another actor in the background. The actor in the foreground becomes almost imperceptible while the actor in the background becomes clear and assumes the dominant position in the scene. This is what happened to you. Your identity as a spirit became blurry and your identity as a body became sharp. In that moment you "became" a body. You did not really change your Self, since your spiritual nature cannot be compromised. But you can come to think of yourself as a body, and a body only. Welcome to planet Earth.

When you "became" a body, you narrowed your world to that revealed by the five senses, a minuscule slice of the vast range of perception available to you. You adopted all the separateness, fear, and hardships that bodies experience, and went into agreement with billions of other souls who believe they are bodies only. You found yourself in a real-life version of the television show *Survivor*, and spent your life trying to avoid getting voted off the island.

That critical moment of immersion into illusion has been called "original sin," the shift in consciousness that caused humanity to fall from a state of grace to the misery of the world. But this was not a sin at all, and in reality the fall never occurred. We are simply dreaming that it did. Original sin was simply an error in perception.

Proponents of the doctrine of original sin have concocted a vast array of gruesome fairy tales about the punishment you deserve simply for being born. Not a word is true. Sin calls for punishment, but error simply requires correction. If your child had a bad dream in which he believed he was a murderer or murdered, you would not punish him when he woke up terrified. You would hold him, comfort him, and explain that it was all just a dream and he is safe. This is precisely what *A Course in Miracles* is communicating to humanity. The cure for the dream of sin is not to tighten the screws of fear that make the dream seem so real. The cure for the dream of sin is awakening.

The initial perceptual shift occurred long ago, but it replicates itself every day. When you slumber at night, your soul goes back to God, and you are renewed as an innocent divine being. In deep sleep you are at peace. Then, when you open your eyes, you slip back into the identity of a body. You remember your aches and pains, the bills you have to pay, the job you wish you didn't have to go to, the repair your car needs, the glut of e-mails in your inbox, your relationship frustrations, the annoying people you have to confront, and all the issues that accompany being a body or an ego. So you are not really waking up. You are going to sleep. You were more awake when you were at peace in deep sleep. What seems like waking is really sleeping; what seems like love is really hate; what seems like life is more like death.

> *Our birth is but a sleep and a forgetting:*
> *The Soul that rises with us, our life's Star,*
> *Hath had elsewhere its setting,*
> *And cometh from afar:*
> *Not in entire forgetfulness,*
> *And not in utter nakedness,*
> *But trailing clouds of glory do we come*
> *From God, who is our home:*
> *Heaven lies about us in our infancy!*
> *Shades of the prison-house begin to close*

*Upon the growing Boy,*
*But he beholds the light, and whence it flows,*
*He sees it in his joy . . .*

— William Wordsworth,
"Ode: Intimations of Immortality
from Recollections of
Early Childhood"

Every day you reenact the shift from unity to separation. But you also have the opportunity to enact the shift from separation to unity. You can use your days to throw off the terrible burden of original sin and reclaim your original innocence. There is no other reason you are here.

> You have not lost your innocence . . . This is the voice you hear, and this the call which cannot be denied . . . And now the way is open, and the journey has an end in sight at last. Be still an instant and go home with Him, and be at peace . . .
>
> — Excerpted from W, Lesson 182

## Food, Sex, and Real Estate

I heard an account by a man who had had a near-death experience. With compelling authority, he told how he had transcended the body and entered a heavenly realm, where he was immersed in pure bliss. For a time he dwelled in golden light. "Then I was sucked back into the sewer," he reported, meaning that he was drawn back to the world defined by the physical senses. "The sewer" is a graphic description of the world, but it often applies—not because that is the nature of the world, but because that is what we have made of it. When you glimpse heaven, Earth as you have known it loses its appeal. Nearly everyone who has had a near-death experience reports that they no longer fear death. They realize that you cannot truly die. Death is not a scary place to go, but a blessed release. Earth, under the advisement of ego, is a far scarier domain.

When we identify with the body only, animal attributes come to the fore and the world becomes a jungle. I saw a nature documentary in which the narrator explained, "Life in the wild is all about food, sex, and real estate." When I shared this description with a seminar audience, a woman said, "Well, not much has changed." At our worst, we act like wild animals. We compete for food, are driven by hormones, wage war over territory, and operate from a survival mentality.

Yet there is more to us than our bodies, and more to the world than savage tendencies. *A Course in Miracles* and all worthy spiritual teachings extricate us from the dense and foreboding jungle most people regard as reality. Our true Self soars far beyond food, sex, and territory. At our core we are love. All acts of kindness, art, and creativity spring from our inherent holiness. We ennoble the world by allowing our godly selves to shine.

In his brilliant book *One Mind,* Dr. Larry Dossey cites the moment when 50-year-old Wesley Autrey stood on a Bronx subway platform and watched a young man succumb to an epileptic seizure, and then fall off the platform into the path of an oncoming train. To onlookers' astonishment, Autrey jumped onto the tracks, covered the man's body, and pressed him into the gutter between the tracks while the train hurtled above both of them. Miraculously, when the train had passed, neither man was injured. The train's undercarriage passed so close to Autrey's head that he emerged with grease marks on his knit cap. People who believe they are bodies only do not jump onto subway tracks to save a stranger's life. Only someone imbued with an awareness of his nature as an immortal spirit would effect such altruism.

When you live as if you are an eternal, invulnerable soul, you raise the bar for all humanity. You transform the world to reflect the dignity it was created to express. You are not required to dive onto subway tracks or become a public hero. Your assignment is the piece of the world you touch. All acts of compassion bring the world closer to heaven.

> The body is the means by which God's Son returns to sanity. Though it was made to fence him into hell without escape, yet has the goal of Heaven been exchanged for

the pursuit of hell. The Son of God extends his hand to reach his brother, and to help him walk along the road with him. Now is the body holy.

— W-Part II.5.4:1-4

## The Holy Spirit's Use of the Ego

By now, you recognize or at least suspect that heeding your ego's dictates has not and will not bring you the happiness you seek. You may have sincerely attempted to rise beyond your ego—but the ego doesn't depart willingly or gracefully. Your kids still drive you up a wall, you worry that your job might disappear, and you know people you wish would take a rocket to Mars and never return. In spite of years of watching Oprah, eating exotic health foods, reading self-help books with lots of bullet points, spilling your guts in therapy, attending pricey seminars, squeezing your body into awkward yoga positions, meditating atop Sedona vortexes, and sitting at the feet of gurus, you still call people names of hidden body parts when they take the parking space you were headed for. Is there any hope for you to find peace of mind?

There is. Even while the ego wages war against the Spirit, the Spirit finds a positive use for the ego. The ego's favorite tool is the intellect, which slices reality into unrecognizable shreds. Yogis say, "The mind is the slayer of the real." Yet the mind can be transformed from an instrument of destruction to one of healing. It can build bombs that kill more people faster, or develop lasers that heal more people faster. When the intellect is employed in service of Spirit, it figures out how to relieve suffering rather than increase it. Dr. Larry Brilliant, Ram Dass, Steve Jobs, and others initiated a project to provide cataract operations for people in underdeveloped countries. This program (seva.org) has now saved the sight of more than three million people. It nobly represents enrolling the intellect as a vehicle for the expression of love.

To master your ego, give it projects that uplift you and others. Put your ego to work making a contribution to humanity rather than sucking from it. I saw graffiti that said KILL YOUR EGO. Don't be so hasty. Such a suggestion assumes that your ego is evil and should be murdered—an idea that proceeds wholly from ego. Rather than killing your ego, subdue it and keep it in its proper place. The ego makes a lousy master, but an extraordinary servant. Think of the ego as a frightened child who has been given a job far bigger than it can handle. It is not equipped to make big decisions or guide your life. That is the function of the Holy Spirit, the part of your mind that remains connected to higher wisdom while you live in the world of separation. Employ the ego to carry out the decisions you make at the level of Spirit. Then all parts of you will be doing what they are supposed to do and everything will get done.

Don't wait for your ego to die before you make your contribution to end suffering. Some of the people who have most profoundly changed the world have egos that would dwarf Godzilla. Yet they harnessed the power of the ego to make others' lives easier. Turn the ego into a miracle worker. It cannot work miracles by itself, but the Holy Spirit can work miracles through it. Then fear will cease to have a hold on you, and you will be at peace.

## What's Your SQ?

The world considers you intelligent if you can manipulate the environment in your body's favor. "What plans do you make that do not involve [the body's] comfort or protection or enjoyment in some way?" (T-18.VII.1:2). IQ tests ask you which house in a picture is different from the others, which number is next in a sequence, and how one cog in a system moves the other cogs. All of this information is related to your ability to control the physical world. It's complex data, and helpful, but not much different from a rat learning to navigate a maze to get to the cheese. (Nothing personal.)

You have never seen any questions on an IQ test related to ethics, morals, virtue, service, or healing. Such tests do not ask: "What person in your life has most contributed to making your life worthwhile?" "If a homeless person asks you for money, how can you best help him?" "What do you answer your child when she asks you, 'Where did Grandma go when she died?' or 'Why don't you and Daddy live together anymore?'" Neither are you asked to explain, "How could God create a world where children starve?"

These questions don't show up because people who believe they are bodies write such tests in order to assess people who wish to survive in a world of bodies. All well and good. Yet as a spiritual being, you have a far broader purpose than to manipulate your environment. You are here to thrive as a soul. It will be a great day when we train children to pass SQ—spiritual quotient—tests. Then we will be teaching genuine intelligence that will advance humanity in the most important way.

> My Self is holy beyond all the thoughts of holiness of which I now conceive. Its shimmering and perfect purity is far more brilliant than is any light that I have ever looked upon. Its love is limitless, with an intensity that holds all things within it, in the calm of quiet certainty.
>
> — W-252.1:1-3

## The Simplest Yet Most Profound Formula

"How do I contribute to end the suffering of humanity?" is the most important question you will ever ask. The answer to that question begins with your answer to the question, "How do I end my own suffering?" If you can find your own way out of pain, you will know how to help other people out of their pain. Until then your efforts are hollow.

Here is a formula for relief from pain that sounds simplistic, but is utterly profound: *Stop doing what hurts you and start doing what heals you.* It is only because you accept—even revere—suffering that it persists. Pain is a result of denial or resistance to your natural self. When you live from your divine nature, suffering will fall away. You will no longer see life as a jungle or live in a realm where survival is at stake. You don't deserve to suffer. No one does. When this truth sinks into your psyche, you will arrive at the tipping point of your spiritual journey, and bleak expectations will give way to the broadest, brightest vision. The world will literally become new and you will live, as Thoreau promised, with "the license of a higher order of beings."

> The world becomes a place of hope, because its only purpose is to be a place where hope of happiness can be fulfilled. And no one stands outside this hope . . .
>
> — T-30.V.2:7-8

# 10

# THE LAST USELESS JOURNEY

An eccentric but likable guy in my town has literally taken upon himself the admonition to bear the cross. Years ago John fashioned a small crucifix out of wood, and since then he regularly walks along the side of a highway carrying the cross. He used to bear the cross on one shoulder while waving and blowing kisses to the folks in passing cars. Local people know John, and many blow kisses back or toot their horn to say hello as they drive past him.

Last year John performed a penance upgrade and fashioned a much larger cross out of PVC pipe. Now he needs two hands to hold the cross rather than one. The sad result of his new format is that his arms are occupied with the cross and he is no longer free to wave and blow kisses. Personally, I was disappointed at his trade-in. I liked him better when he was broadcasting love. He looked like he was having more fun. When your arms and shoulders are taken up carrying a cross, you can't give the love you are capable of sharing when they are free. Self-imposed suffering is not a gift to the world. It renders you less capable of loving, not more.

Many religions and belief systems accept suffering as an inescapable reality and even glorify it. Christians sing with romantic masochism of bearing the old rugged cross. Hindus justify poverty and disease as the paying off of karma. And the answer to the question, "How many Jewish mothers does it take to change a lightbulb?" is, "None—but that's all right; I'll just sit here in the dark." By a bizarre twist of reason, pain has been forged into a breastplate for the downtrodden.

A *Course in Miracles* finds no purpose in pain. It tells us that there is no virtue in suffering, and you cannot redeem hardship for liberation. The Course boldly declares that the thorny path has not been set by God, and misery is optional. Torturing ourselves or others for any reason is a sick story we have made up. None of it is necessary.

## Life After Sacrifice

I have often pondered the choice of the crucifix as the symbol for Christianity. Jesus Christ lived for 33 years, we are told. He taught, ministered, and healed publicly for the last three years of his earthly journey, during which he performed miracles, redeemed souls, and transformed lives. The light he generated has radiated across two millennia and continues to renew the spirit of those it touches. Finally, Jesus was murdered on a crucifix, impaled for less than the time the sun rose and set. Yet for all the healing Jesus achieved, the power he demonstrated, and the blessings he bestowed, his life is commemorated by the method of his death. A friend of mine suggested, "If Jesus Christ lived during our time and met the same fate, for the next 2,000 years people would be walking around with little gold electric chairs hanging from chains around their necks."

Unsettling as this proposal may be, it makes us pause to consider the inappropriate veneration for pain that has crept into a religion based on the teachings of a healer. How bizarre that we commemorate the day of his death by calling it "Good Friday." The resurrection is far more significant. What an improved role model Jesus would provide if his primary image were that of a shining face and arms open to embrace. How empowered we would be to know him in health and life, rather than death. Then we would be moved to lay aside our own crosses and fulfill the purpose Jesus claimed for himself, and wishes for all of us: "I came that they may have life, and have it abundantly" (John 10:10).

The message of the crucifixion is perfectly clear: *Teach only love, for that is what you are.* If you interpret the crucifixion in any other way, you are using it as a weapon for assault rather than as the call for peace for which it was intended.

— T-6.I.13:1-2, T-6.I.14:1

## Vicarious Illumination

I saw a film that depicted Jesus returning to the world as a modern man. Whenever Jesus performed a healing, the movie showed him wincing or grasping a part of his body suddenly distressed, implying that he had sacrificed his well-being to accomplish the healing. The message was that giving healing damages the healer, and service begets suffering; for the patient to gain, Jesus had to lose. *Nothing could be further from the truth.* The filmmakers clearly did not understand the process of true healing, and they did Jesus a disservice in this portrayal. Jesus did not go into pain with the people he healed. Instead, they came into wellness with him. In genuine healing, the healer loses nothing and both healer and patient benefit. "[Miracles] bring more love both to the giver *and* the receiver" (T-1.I.9:3).

The theological term for removing the pain of others by taking it on yourself is "vicarious atonement." This concept is the fantasy of humanity, not the truth of God. You cannot get sad enough to make someone else happy. You cannot get poor enough to make someone else rich. You cannot get sick enough to make someone else well. Your pain cannot buy another's peace. Your joy and establishment in wellness will help him more.

*Vicarious illumination* is a model of healing far closer to truth than vicarious atonement. There is still a flaw in the premise, for you cannot do something for another person that only she can do for herself. But the idea that your happiness can help someone else more than your suffering is a far more practical healing tool than the notion that your loss becomes someone else's gain. When one of us loses, we all lose. When one of us gains, we all gain. "When I am healed I am not healed alone" (W, Lesson 137). For this reason, your most powerful contribution to humanity is your happiness. Suffering is an old and tired story. Been there, done that, bought the T-shirt.

True healers do not suffer with or for their patients. Instead, they invite their patients to meet them on higher ground. When you touch a lit candle to the wick of an unlit candle, the original flame is not diminished. Instead, it expands. The parent is not weakened by the progeny. Light is not less for shining. Your wellness cannot remove the happiness of another, and your sorrow cannot bring him joy. Brokenness is not the road to wholeness. Only wholeness will take you there.

## Jesus Comments on the Crucifixion

In *A Course in Miracles,* Jesus makes many references to the events of his life as recorded in the New Testament. He offers liberating reframes for moments we have traditionally interpreted through maudlin mind-sets. Here is what he says about the crucifixion:

> The journey to the cross should be the last "useless journey." Do not dwell upon it, but dismiss it as accomplished. If you can accept it as your own last useless journey, you are also free to join my resurrection. Until you do so your life is indeed wasted. It merely re-enacts the separation, the loss of power, the futile attempts of the ego at reparation, and finally the crucifixion of the body, or death. Such repetitions are endless until they are voluntarily given up. Do not make the pathetic error of "clinging to the old rugged cross." The only message of the crucifixion is that you can overcome the cross. Until then you are free to crucify yourself as often as you choose. This is not the gospel I intended to offer you. We have another journey to undertake . . .
>
> — T-4.IN.3

Jesus never asked us to go on the cross with him and he did not die for your sins. That premise is faulty because Christ is deathless and you have no sins. Instead, he lives for your innocence. He is the model of a man who recognized his innate divinity, the same godliness you own. He does not want you to emulate his crucifixion. He wants you to magnify his resurrection. You don't need to experience crucifixion to gain resurrection. There are easier ways to get to heaven.

**Love does not kill to save.**

— T-13.IN.3.3

## The Use and Uselessness of Illness

Pain is most apparent in physical illness, which we have been taught is a fact of life. "You get old, you get sick, and you die," we learn by word, image, and model. "The only sure things in life are death and taxes." *A Course in Miracles* disagrees. It teaches us that illness is a choice we make. So is healing. When we find no value in illness and we withdraw our investment in it, it will disappear.

"If pain and illness are optional," you ask, "why would anyone choose them?" The answer is: *perceived* payoff. We all do what we *believe* brings us benefit. Here are some common perceived payoffs for illness:

**1. You get excused from school, work, and doing things you don't want to do.**

When you didn't want to go to elementary school, you either faked being sick or, if you had liberal parents, they let you stay home because you wanted to. The next day you brought a note to your teacher: "Please excuse Linda for being absent from school yesterday. She had a fever." As your teacher nodded and sent you to your desk without punishment, you learned that illness buys you reprieve. If you had brought your teacher a note saying, "Please excuse Linda for being absent from school yesterday. She finds school boring and she preferred to stay home," you (and your parents) would have gotten into lots of trouble. So you learned that it was more expedient to be sick or play sick than tell a truth that might cause upset or get you in trouble. "Sickness is a defense against the truth" (W, Lesson 136). At some point that dynamic established itself at an unconscious level, and illness assumed the power to excuse.

The same process replicates itself in adult life. If, for example, you have to cancel a flight, the only way to get your money back is to produce a note from a doctor saying that you were ill. Doctors' notes are the GET OUT OF JAIL FREE card in the Monopoly game of life. But your freedom is not really without cost. To keep the exemption in force, you must bear pain. Is it worth it?

There are easier and more direct ways to say no than to play or be sick. A coaching client told me that after her divorce she had gained a lot of weight and now she wanted to lose it. I asked her, "What benefit do you find in keeping the weight on?"

"I believe it makes me less attractive to men," she replied. "The end of my marriage and my divorce were horrible, and I am not ready for a relationship."

"Then perhaps you could simply choose to not be in a relationship without needing the weight to say 'no' for you," I suggested.

She loved that approach as a more direct and practical tool than keeping the weight on as a defense against relationship pain.

### 2. You get attention and sympathy.
When you were sick as a kid, your mom stayed home from work to take care of you. She brought you food in bed, you got to watch TV during the day, and you got ice cream for dessert. Adult illnesses earn different kinds of attention, but the dynamic is identical.

### 3. You get money.
Insurance companies will give you money for being injured. Insurance policies spell this out before you even sign on the dotted line. The loss of an arm is worth up to $440,000 in some states,

a big toe up to $90,000, and burns to 20 percent of your body can add $100,000 to your bank account. I am not suggesting that if someone is disabled, they should not receive financial assistance and other forms of support. I *am* suggesting that when you are rewarded with money for being sick (usually in more subtle ways than those listed above), sickness becomes more attractive and can even become addictive.

The tragic hitch of being paid for illness is that at some point the payoff for illness begins to outweigh the reward for wellness. If you have to prove to a government agency or insurance company that you are disabled, you are also proving it to yourself. Beware of the case you make to others, for you are making the case also to yourself, and your experience will bear out your argument.

If you can prove someone hurt you, then you can get them to give you money—or at least you can try. Much of our legal system is based on financial reparation for victimization. Being a victim in our culture can be very lucrative. Yet ACIM tells us, "I am not the victim of the world I see" (W, Lesson 31). How empty would our courts be if we each assumed responsibility for our own experience?

When I visited Peru, a child with a twisted arm approached our tour group and asked for alms. Generously, we gave. Later our tour director informed us that some parents in underdeveloped countries maim their children so they will fetch more money begging.

For a fascinating public exhibition of a treasured wound (a concept introduced in an earlier chapter), consider the famous "A-bomb dome" in Hiroshima, Japan. In the wake of the horrendous atomic bombing at the end of World War II, one building in Hiroshima remained standing, its structure reduced to a concrete shell and steel girders. Since the war, the A-bomb dome has stood as a grim symbol of the city's infamous disaster.

In the 1960s, a group of Hiroshima citizens launched a movement to finally take down the skeleton of the building and put to rest the daily reminder of hell. Another group protested, arguing that the A-bomb dome had become a landmark, drawing many thousands of tourists every year to visit the site of the disaster.

Those tourists brought many millions of yen to Hiroshima's economy, and without it the city might be set back financially. After a heated debate, the city council decided to keep the A-bomb dome. To this day it stands as the central symbol of Hiroshima. Every tourist guide and map features the blasted wreck on its cover, and photographers bathe it in romantic lights for special effects. The city's greatest wound has become its most valued treasure. The city earns money in exchange for living in the shadow of a horrid memory.

**4. You get revenge or to be "right" by making someone else guilty.**

ACIM asks us, "Do you prefer that you be right or happy?" (T-29.VII.1:9). The ego justifies its position by calling other people wrong. Yet it gains nothing and loses everything.

I saw a documentary about a man who believed that his mortgage company was overcharging him on his monthly payments. After fighting with them for a long time, he sent the company an angry letter threatening that he would kill anyone who tried to come on his property and take his home away from him. The mortgage company turned his letter over to the authorities, who arrested and tried the man and put him in jail. From jail he continued his vendetta. The documentary showed him talking to his wife on the telephone from prison, telling her what new tactic he was going to try to defeat the mortgage company. Finally she broke into tears and told him, "When are you going to give up this war? I just wish you would come home."

This is, after a fashion, what God is saying to us: "Would you please just quit having to be right about what is wrong, and come home?"

## The Critical Shift

When wellness becomes more appealing than illness, you become a beacon of healing for others. We all know people who are happy no matter what happens to them. Their attitude supersedes their circumstances. A movie reviewer described a film character as "the kind of guy who has no troubles because he doesn't want any."

My friend Jennifer Allen is such a person. Wife, mother of five, businesswoman, and spiritual explorer, Jennifer just keeps choosing peace. As a result, she has limitless energy. She once gave me a massage with one hand while she held her one-year-old daughter in her other arm.

At one time I saw Jennifer at a conference. As we sat in a lecture hall waiting for a program to begin, she showed me the final draft of a book she had written on parenting, and asked me to have a look at it during my free time. "Please take good care of this book," she told me. "It is my only copy and it contains lots of original photos that cannot be replaced." When I saw Jennifer later that day, she asked me if I had had a chance to look at the book. Suddenly I realized that I had left the book in the auditorium. Highly embarrassed, I told her what had happened. Instead of getting upset, Jennifer shrugged her shoulders and said, "Well, maybe the book wasn't meant to be published." I was stunned by her willingness to choose peace in the face of a situation that would severely upset most people. We went back to the auditorium and asked the custodian if he had found the book. Fortunately, he had. I believe the purpose of that experience was to teach me that peace is a choice we make.

I know other people who have walked away from bad marriages without engaging in a divorce battle, who have refused to sue when they might have made a case, and who have quit high-paying but grueling corporate jobs because keeping their soul alive was more important than financing their boat. Then there was William, a young man who had been diagnosed with cancer at age 17. Years ago he came to a seminar and recounted, "One day when I was scheduled for chemotherapy, I found out there was a Grateful Dead concert in my city that night. I decided to have some fun instead of get my treatment, so I went to the concert. Soon afterward I was pronounced cancer-free."

The body is *a representation* of mind and emotions. It is more liquid than solid, and has an astounding capacity to re-form itself into its natural healthy pattern. No limiting condition need be permanent. At any moment you can change your mind, which leads to transformed circumstances. Your body doesn't cause your thoughts. It is a *result* of them.

## Compassion Trumps Upset

The right-thinking mind regards pain and difficulty as a call for kindness and compassion. I attended a concert by the Brothers Cazimero, two talented and well-loved Hawaiian musicians. Early in the evening one of the brothers, Roland, fell ill and had to leave the stage. Suddenly his brother, Robert, found himself onstage in front of a thousand people without his partner, unable to perform the two-hour repertoire they had rehearsed. He had to wing it.

The audience was quite disappointed. Here we had paid for tickets and come out for this big event, and it wasn't going to happen. We wanted Robert *and* Roland, not just Robert. Instead of complaining, however, the audience mounted massive support for both brothers. People called out, "We love you, Roland!" as he left the stage. We applauded wildly for Robert as he tried to patch together a concert. He made some chord errors, and one of the male hula dancers in his ensemble had his costume nearly fall off onstage while the troupe improvised a dance. None of that mattered. We all understood this was an emergency situation, and everyone pulled together to make the best of it. By the end of the evening, the musical presentation was not at all what we had expected, but the concert hall was filled with celebration. After the finale, Robert received a standing ovation. Many in the audience inwardly held Roland in prayer. Higher Mind reframed an awkward situation as a call for love, and transformed the event. As a result, the evening was far more rewarding than if we had simply heard the concert as planned.

## The End of Terrorism

Humility is a virtue. Humiliation is not. Humbling yourself means allowing God to bring greater life to the world through you rather than letting yourself be a pawn in the ego's quest for blood. God champions your wellness and is doing everything He can to promote it. All else is a tragic misunderstanding of the will of God.

The world has become obsessed with terrorism. Governments spend trillions of dollars on wars against terrorists, our beloved sons and daughters come home in caskets, and millions of innocent people are forced to undress in airports in order to ride on an airplane. Has it ever occurred to you that this is not how humanity was intended to live? Yet we can learn from even this most insane of scenarios: "All things are lessons God would have me learn" (W, Lesson 193).

The answer to terrorism, personal and global, is found in the very place it lives: the fearful heart. Terrorism will end when we refuse to be terrified. The most insidious criminal is the *inner* terrorist, the part of your mind that bullies you or accepts bullying by others. An agitator in your psyche attempts to keep you small by encasing you in a circle of fear. You believe you are a tiny human body, alone, defenseless, and subject to the evil of the world. You believe people can hurt you without your permission, and you are powerless to create the life you yearn for. You believe you must go to a job you hate and tolerate obnoxious bosses, mean-spirited co-workers, and whiny customers. You accept that you must put up with demeaning relationships, struggle to survive, prove yourself to dead relatives, and hack your way through the jungle of life. Such inner terrorism is far more destructive to life on the planet than those who blow up cars and buildings. Psychic self-destruction turns bright, competent children with genius potential into hollow-eyed drones trudging through mind-numbing schools and then life-sucking jobs. The inner terrorist twists humanity into a writhing mass of fear, looking everywhere for love and finding it nowhere. So the world becomes a mockery of the heaven it was intended to be.

To all of this, *A Course in Miracles* says, "Peace to such foolishness!" (W-190.4:1). It assures us that as children of a loving, caring God, we deserve better. It emphatically tells us that crucifixion of self or others is not the will of God. "Perhaps you have misunderstood His plan, for He would never offer pain to you"

(W-135.18:2). The will of God is entirely, utterly, eternally, only love. ACIM assures us that this is our will as well, therefore it must be done on Earth as it is in heaven.

All journeys to all crosses are useless. There is a way to live that is closer to God. It is time for us to claim resurrection without crucifixion. The hilarious Monty Python movie *Life of Brian* concludes with a group of men hanging on crucifixes at the time of Jesus. Together they sing and whistle "Always Look on the Bright Side of Life." While the humor is dark, there is a lesson that goes beyond the film: The crucified didn't need to be there in the first place. Torture is a paradigm we have outgrown. Christ would not take that journey again, and neither need you.

> He will remove all faith that you have placed in pain, disaster, suffering and loss. He gives you vision which can look beyond these grim appearances, and can behold the gentle face of Christ in all of them. You will no longer doubt that only good can come to you who are beloved of God . . .
>
> — W-151.10:1-3

# 11

# BEYOND MAGIC

When I took a group to Egypt for a spiritual pilgrimage, a member named Gloria found an unusual stone at the base of a pyramid. The pink, round rock glowed with a mystical light, and as she held it in her hand she felt an intense energy emanating from it. She wondered if it had been used by ancient priests for healing, or perhaps adorned the headdress of a pharaoh.

Gloria stole off to a quiet place and began to meditate, her fingers clutching the stone. In her mind she asked for images of the sacred ceremonies the stone may have been used for many centuries ago. Instantly she beheld pictures of Egyptians in ornate robes chanting and healing on the banks of the Nile. Long-buried visions began to surface; this extraordinary moment was clearly the reason Gloria had been guided to travel halfway around the globe.

After a few minutes, this inspired pilgrim was amazed to feel the stone getting softer. A sense of alchemy arose; perhaps this gem was a shape-shifter, transforming in the aura of prayer. As Gloria continued to meditate, the stone became even softer, to the point of being gooey. Unable to wait longer, she looked down to see what the stone had become. Long pink strands were stretching across her hand and hanging down toward the ground. The "stone" was a wad of bubble gum.

This true story demonstrates the power of the mind to create an experience. Gloria intended to connect with the mystical tradition of that ancient culture, and she did. The stone/bubble gum was her chosen vehicle to deliver the experience she sought. Would Gloria's experience have been more valid if she had picked up an actual jewel from the pharaoh's headdress? Not necessarily.

Neither gems nor chewing gum create experience. Mind creates experience. All of life is mind over matter.

## Where Real Magic Lives

"Magic," according to *A Course in Miracles,* is the belief that an object outside of yourself has the power to heal you or hurt you; that the environment, rather than our thoughts, is the source of our experience. Yet we are told:

> . . . you believe you are sustained by everything but God. Your faith is placed in the most trivial and insane symbols; pills, money, "protective" clothing, influence, prestige, being liked, knowing the "right" people, and an endless list of forms of nothingness that you endow with magical powers. All these things are your replacements for the Love of God.
>
> — W-50.1:2-3,50.2:1

Magic is the misappropriation of authority from the inner spirit to an external force. But *there is no external force.* You are not in the world. The world is in you. Everything that seems to be in the world is in your mind. There is nothing outside of you.

The world entertains endless beliefs in magic. We believe in medicine, money, possessions, esoteric sciences, gurus, healers, amulets, exotic lands, sacred sites, rituals, exercise, makeup, matchmakers, marriage, babies, schools, real estate, corporations, technology, governments, and much more. The theme of magic is, "I don't have what I need to be happy. That person, tool, or technique will wave its wand, and I will import what I am missing." Then we set out on a long fruitless quest for something outside ourselves to give us what we don't already own. Magic is a projection of our innate power onto a neutral object. We suffer only from displacement of divinity.

Because the ego doesn't want to hear that its domain is fabricated of smoke and mirrors, you may feel insulted to hear that your favorite form of magic is not inherently powerful. "Dr. _____'s seminar saved my life!" you exclaim. Yes, it did. But it was not really the seminar that saved your life. It was *you*. You were ready and willing for transformation, and you used the seminar as a permission slip to give yourself what you wanted and needed. You could have done it without the seminar.

But don't shoot the Course just yet. It doesn't require you to give up your Zumba class, herbal supplements, or trip to Machu Picchu. It just wants you to recognize that these methods are tools, not saviors. The real magic is inside you.

## No Laws but God's

One of ACIM's most profound Workbook Lessons, "I am under no laws but God's" (W, Lesson 76), calls us to rise above magic and claim the real source of our well-being:

> You really think that you would starve unless you have stacks of green paper strips and piles of metal discs. You really think a small round pellet or some fluid pushed into your veins through a sharpened needle will ward off disease and death. You really think you are alone unless another body is with you.
>
> It is insanity that thinks these things. You call them laws, and put them under different names in a long catalogue of rituals that have no use and serve no purpose. You think you must obey the "laws" of medicine, of economics and of health. Protect the body, and you will be saved.
>
> These are not laws, but madness . . . There are no laws except the laws of God . . .
>
> — Excerpted from W, Lesson 76

How liberating to consider that you don't need anything outside yourself to be healed or happy! What a relief to not have to pursue endless books, classes, teachers, diets, travels, gadgets, and techniques to find peace! How much money you will save on therapy and seminars! The ego tells us that heaven is a place to get to. The Course assures us that we carry heaven with us.

Begin to free yourself from the shackles of magic by first noticing, then questioning, then challenging any beliefs you hold that some external force or source is doing it *to* you or *for* you. Does a doctor heal you, or do you make the choice to be healed? Does a certain balance in your bank account provide security, or are you safe no matter how many dollars to your name? How many educational degrees does it take for you to be credible? Who must agree with you in order for you to feel validated? Do you need a partner to experience love, or is love already where you stand? Few people in our culture question magic. Fewer move beyond it. If you are reading these words, you are being called to walk through the veil of illusion that keeps the world but a miniature of its true potential. Buddha asked, "If you do not get it from yourself, where will you go for it?" All the authority you will ever need is seeded within your soul. Look there and nowhere else.

## The Real Physician

Over millennia, people have been healed by methods that to the modern mind seem like primitive quackery. Just 150 years ago if you went to a physician complaining of a sore throat, he might have drained nearly all the blood from your body. If you were a sexually frustrated wife in Victorian England, you would visit a doctor's office, where he would relieve you via manual manipulation. (The electric vibrator was invented by a physician whose arm grew sore after healing so many wives.) In the early 20th century, phrenology, the science of reading the bumps on your head, was considered a valid diagnostic tool. Even today orthodox acupuncturists might prescribe that you affix leeches to your face to restore skin tone, place razor blades on your tongue to stimulate your gums, or eat a ground-up centipede.

Bizarre as these methods may seem, they have worked for many people. *Belief is powerful.* One might wonder how a doctor or healer of the future might regard our healing methods today. In the Star Trek movie *The Voyage Home,* Dr. McCoy returns from the future to visit a hospital of 20th-century Earth. When he observes the methods used to treat patients, his eyes bulge and he exclaims, "Unbelievable!"

Yet all methods are believable because people believe in them. Every method works for someone. The method does not bestow the healing. The belief does.

*A Course in Miracles* tells us that no method at all is necessary. We can be healed simply by choosing to be healed. A profound passage in the Manual for Teachers lays out this principle in stark terms:

> Who is the physician? Only the mind of the patient himself. The outcome is what he decides that it is. Special agents seem to be ministering to him, yet they but give form to his own choice. He chooses them in order to bring tangible form to his desires. And it is this they do, and nothing else. They are not actually needed at all. The patient could merely rise up without their aid and say, "I have no use for this." There is no form of sickness that would not be cured at once.
>
> — M-5.II.2.5-13

*A Course in Miracles* tells us that we have the capacity, the power, and the right to be healed if we so choose. Choice is the cornerstone of all experience. Remove from your mind all the preconditions you believe are required before you can be well, and the healing you thought was distant or impossible is available now.

## According to Your Belief

Does the insubstantiality of methods mean you should never see a doctor, take a pill, or go on a juice fast? Not necessarily. A key factor in healing is to *work with the belief system you trust.* If you believe in a surgeon, shaman, hypnotist, or juicing instructor, and your intention is to be healed, the treatment will work. Use your positive beliefs to leverage you beyond the negative ones.

A famous self-help author did an experiment to demonstrate the belief factor in healing. He offered two identical weekend seminars in a major U.S. city, one month after the other. For the first seminar he charged $50, and 300 people attended. For the second seminar he charged $500, and 300 other people attended. The participants at both workshops experienced equally successful results. The people who believed that a self-help seminar should be inexpensive attended the first weekend. Those who believed that if a seminar is expensive, it must be valuable, attended the second program. Payment does not determine healing; mind does. My mentor Hilda did not charge anything for all the healing sessions and classes she gave for nearly 30 years, and she transformed the lives of many thousands of people. Other organizations teach that clients will benefit from services only if they make a significant financial investment. They attract thousands of students willing to pay high tuitions over many years, and also create positive results. "Be it done unto you according to your belief" (Matthew 9:29).

## Altars of Faith

*All* healing is faith healing. We all have faith in *something*. Everyone is attending the church they believe in because belief builds churches, including those that have nothing to do with religion. Science, money, sex, food, and politics are churches because people believe in them and worship at their altars. All dedication is a statement of belief in the power to which you subscribe.

If you need healing, go confidently to the object of your faith. See a coach, doctor, priest, shaman, massage therapist, Reiki master, or friend you trust. If nature brings you peace, retreat to the forest. Stretch in your yoga class. Commit to the diet that makes you feel the best. It matters not if anyone else understands you, agrees with you, or joins you. What matters is that you act in alignment with your beliefs.

Since most of us don't have perfect faith in Spirit alone, we may need to resort to more mechanical means of healing. Jesus used the belief systems of his patients to stimulate their transformation. He rubbed mud on a blind man's eyes and told him to rinse it off and he would be healed. The man acceded, and he regained his sight (John 9:6–11). Jesus knew there was no magical power in the mud. But the man's belief required an object through which healing could transpire. So Jesus compassionately gave him that object. Jesus was more interested in bringing the man relief than in waiting for him to have perfect faith. Acting on partial faith leads to perfect faith. Partial faith *is* perfect in the sense that your belief is whole in the moment you mobilize it.

ACIM tells us that all that is required for a miracle is a "little willingness" (T-18.IV). Jesus used the symbol of a mustard seed to illustrate the power of even a little faith. The tiniest of seeds grows into a mighty bush. Just point your mind in the direction where your faith lives, and success will ensue.

Sincerity will take you farther than dogma. What heals someone else may not heal you because it was that person's faith that healed that person. Likewise, it is your own faith that will heal you. Faith is more powerful than action because action is a tool of faith. Action without faith is impotent. When your actions are in harmony with your faith, you are in integrity with yourself and you will achieve your goal.

## Perfect Love Casts Out Disease

If you cannot claim perfect faith, claim perfect love. Belief in love is the most effective faith, because God is love. When you love sincerely, the power of the entire universe is behind you.

All disease is a denial of love, and all denial of love is fear. When the Bible tells us, "Perfect love casts out fear" (John 4:18), it is also teaching that perfect love casts out disease. You don't have to have a title, degrees, or fancy techniques to heal. You just have to genuinely love. I know of a woman who dedicated her life to healing women with eating disorders. She took emaciated women from hospitals and cared for them in her home. She held them in her arms, looked into their eyes, and told them, "You are a beautiful, precious angel. You are a blessing to the world. I love you, and I want you to live and be happy." She understood that the inability to receive food, the most basic necessity of physical life, represents the inability to receive love, the fundamental necessity of spiritual life. When she gave those women love, she was healing them at the core level. This healer had a huge success rate, and restored to wellness many women who could not be cured by other healing modalities. Love is the ultimate healer. Without love, nothing lives. With love, all things thrive.

Love heals because it reminds us of who we were before we were taught we needed something from outside to make us enough. Faith in outer sources yields temporary success, but faith in our inner Source yields permanent success. The fear-based mind seeks power *from* the world, while the love-based mind brings power *to* the world. When you accept your inherent majesty rather than attributing unmerited power to external agents, you will perform miracles that cannot be explained in any terms the world understands.

> Dismiss all foolish magical beliefs today, and hold your mind in silent readiness to hear the Voice that speaks the truth to you . . . Magic imprisons, but the laws of God make free.

> — W-76.9:2,7:5

# Why Is the Course Written in Psychological Language?

ACIM is filled with terms straight out of a psychology class. *Ego, projection, defense mechanisms, attack thoughts, dissociation, resistance, the power of the mind,* and *unconscious motivation* are foundational terms and themes running through the Course. Is Jesus Christ a Freudian?

No, but Dr. Helen Schucman, the channel for the Course, was a psychotherapist whose training, practice, and teaching were founded on those terms. In the process of channeling, the source of the material transmits blocks of thought, or concepts, to the channel, who interprets and expresses them according to the mind-set with which he or she is familiar. The Course was recorded by Dr. Schucman in the English language because that is the one she spoke. If she were French, the Course would have arrived in French. If the Course came to an artist, the material would appear in the form of a painting; to a musician, a symphony; to a mathematician, a formula. Since Dr. Schucman was a psychologist, the Course showed up in "psychologese." For this reason, *A Course in Miracles* is sometime referred to as "spiritual psychotherapy."

Even more than Western culture believes in Christianity, it believes in psychology. Psychology and self-help books consistently top bestseller lists, and many people who experience mental or emotional distress turn to a psychologist for help. Psychiatrists have the power to dispense medications and commit people to mental institutions. In many ways psychology is the religion of our time; in countries where religion does not thrive, psychology does. God finds us where we live and speaks to us in the language of our belief. ". . . a miracle, to attain its full efficacy, must be expressed in a language that the recipient can understand without fear" (T-2.IV.5:3).

The word *psychology* derives from the Greek word *psyche,* which means "soul." True psychology, then, pierces beyond the study of the mind alone, and reaches us at the core of our being. Genuine healing is holistic. The healing of the body proceeds from the healing of the mind, and the healing of the mind proceeds from the healing of the soul. *A Course in Miracles* accomplishes the deepest level of healing, earning it the appellation "psychology" in the truest sense of the word.

# 12

# YOUR IMPECCABLE GUIDE

One night the neighbor of the Sufi rascal-sage Nasrudin came home to find Nasrudin kneeling under a streetlamp, searching for something in the grass. "What are you looking for?" the neighbor asked.

"I dropped my house key," Nasrudin replied.

"Then I'll help you," the neighbor offered. He, too, got down on his knees and began to finger through the turf.

After half an hour without success the neighbor asked, "Do you remember where you were standing when you dropped it?"

"Over there," Nasrudin answered, pointing to a dark spot 20 yards from the streetlight.

"Then why are you looking here?" asked the neighbor, befuddled.

"There's more light over here."

It seems attractive to look for answers where others are searching or where they tell us we should look. Popular opinion urges us to travel to distant lands to ferret out remote sages, unearth ancient relics, and stand on power vortexes. While such journeys make for titillating adventures, the real criterion by which to evaluate such a trek is, "Am I now closer to peace?" If so, your seeking has been worthwhile. If not, you must reevaluate where and how you are looking. The ego's motto is "Seek and do *not* find" (T-12.IV.1:4). It denies the reality of love and regards healing as a threat. Any answer is acceptable to the ego as long as it does not work. Is there another place to look that will *end* searching rather than *reinforce* it?

*A Course in Miracles* assures us that we have an impeccable guide *within* us, qualified and available to answer all of our questions, extricate us from gnarly thickets, and lead us to our cherished goals. The Course identifies this guide as the Holy Spirit. The Holy Spirit is the part of your mind that remains connected to the Mind of God even while another part of the mind is immersed in the illusion of separation. The Course regards the Holy Spirit as a person, the one true friend you can trust, who loves you more than the ego ever will. He knows the truth about you, understands where real help lives, and is generous in his willingness to illuminate your path.

The Holy Spirit works like a night-light in a darkened house. The moment daylight dims, a sensor turns the night-light on. This process ensures there will always be light. The darker the outer world becomes, the brighter the inner light glows. God would not leave us to flounder in a dimension of error.

The Course urges us to turn difficult situations over to the Holy Spirit's care. This requires humility and trust. If you are hell-bent on letting the ego run the show, you will attempt a multitude of solutions that don't work, resort to brute force, and find endless reasons to justify your limits. But if you value peace more than arrogance and success more than struggle, you will turn to Higher Power for help and be open to receive it. And it will come.

> The Thought of God protects you, cares for you, makes soft your resting place and smooth your way, lighting your mind with happiness and love. Eternity and everlasting life shine in your mind, because the Thought of God has left you not, and still abides with you.
>
> — W-165.2:6-7

## Sure Signs

One of the Course's principles of miracles is, "His Voice will direct you very specifically. You will be told all you need to know" (T-1.I.4:2–3). How reassuring to know that we don't have to figure it all out by ourselves!

At one time I was considering purchasing a remote rural property. As I walked the land with my real estate agent, I liked the property, but I had an odd negative feeling about it. So I asked Holy Spirit for a sign as to whether or not to pursue the purchase. As we were about to exit the property, two tough-looking guys with big dogs stopped us. They told us that they were the neighbors and they didn't want anyone living there. They claimed they had the water rights to the land and would not give them to anyone else. And they went on and on. Since I had no interest in living next to such unwelcoming neighbors, I had my sign, and I let the property go. I later found and purchased an even better property with gracious neighbors.

At another time my beloved Dee and I were traveling in Japan with a friend who offered to show us around the countryside. Before the tour she took us to an organic restaurant for lunch, where we were seated next to an American couple living in Japan. They suggested we visit a certain Zen temple in the mountains. We went to the temple and found it to be extraordinarily inspiring, a series of 30 temples ascending the slopes, surrounded by a forest of tens of thousands of 500-year-old cedar trees reaching high into the heavens. The grace of the temples' architecture and the tranquility of the space were beyond stunning. I wanted to stay there forever. That visit proved to be the highlight of that trip to Japan, and I now hold that space in my heart as a vision of heaven on Earth. I marvel at the synchronicity of how we were guided to that place. It is not something we could have engineered. It was a God job. The Holy Spirit works through people. At any time you may serve as a voice of guidance for another person, and anyone might serve as a channel through which the Holy Spirit guides you.

## Just Show Me

"Please show me" is one of the most powerful prayers you can speak. But you must be open to Spirit's guidance rather than telling God how to run the show. "Please show me, as long as your answer is the one I think it should be," is a self-limiting prayer.

Very often the Holy Spirit has a plan and intention for us that goes far beyond any we could conceive for ourselves. This is why the Lesson "I do not perceive my own best interests" (W, Lesson 24) comes early in the Workbook. As much as the ego would like you to believe it knows what is best for you, it doesn't. When all of the ego's plans have tanked, the Holy Spirit stands ready to throw you a life preserver. Better yet, turn to the Holy Spirit *before* you fall off the ship. You can avoid painful trials and errors by inviting Spirit to guide you at the *outset* of your decision-making process. Your impeccable guide will make decisions for you in ways far more rewarding than you can make for yourself. Twelve-step programs attribute the healing of addiction to partnering with Higher Power, and rightfully so. God can and will do everything for you that you cannot do for yourself.

> . . . hear but the Voice for God and for your Self . . . He will direct your efforts, telling you exactly what to do, how to direct your mind, and when to come to Him in silence, asking for His sure direction and His certain Word.
>
> — W.Ep.3:2-3

## *Where the Guru Lives*

One of my Japanese clients went to a psychic, who told her that she would one day marry an American lawyer, he would cheat on her, and the marriage would end in divorce. Although this client is a well-educated professional, this "reading" threw her into a tizzy. I told her that no psychic is 100 percent accurate. Important choices rest in our own hands: "The power of decision is my own" (W, Lesson 152). Mature psychics do not present events to come as cast in stone. At best, they may identify themes, patterns, and likelihoods. At any moment you can make a new choice and set a new direction. I told my client that her destiny depends on her intention more than any externally imposed fate. We construct our future by the consciousness we hold.

Human counselors can help us, but only if their advice resonates with our inner guidance. Never do anything just because a consultant tells you to do it. Follow outer advice only if your *internal* consultant resonates. Wise psychics do not seek or accept the power you are inclined to bestow upon them. Instead, they push you back on your inner resources. One of my favorite book titles is by psychic Dougall Fraser. It reminds us, *But You Knew That Already.*

When faced with any decision, imagine that you know already. Your task is not to roam the earth seeking someone smarter than you to tell you what to do. Your task is to dive into your heart and remember what you know. The ultimate guru lives within you. That is why the word *guru* is spelled g-u-r-u: *"gee, you are you."*

## Your Best Friend's Voice

You can discern between the advice of the Holy Spirit and that of the ego by noticing the feeling or energy the voice or advice generates. Spirit is founded in love. The ego operates from fear. Love feels good, light, and peaceful and brings relief. Fear feels bad, heavy, and limiting and deepens distress. Love and fear are not entities, but *energies, frequencies,* or *streams of experience.*

Imagine that Susan is your best friend. Someone you do not know phones you and says, "Hi, this is Susan. Something really important has come up. I need you to meet me at Starbucks in an hour."

Would you go?

Of course not. You *know* your best friend's voice and the energy it carries. That voice is familiar to you, comfortable, and trustworthy. Soon into a conversation with an impostor, you would realize that although this person says she is your best friend, *she is not.*

Now imagine that Susan phones you and does not say her name. "Something really important has come up," she tells you. "Meet me at Starbucks in an hour."

Would you go?

Certainly. You know your friend's voice and her energy. She did not even need to speak her name. You discerned on an energetic level that it was she. That felt good and you responded.

This is precisely how the voices of love and fear operate, and how to respond. The voice of love is your best friend. When it speaks, it feels familiar, safe, empowering, and trustworthy, like you are coming home. It is a pleasure to hear it and act on it. It works and gets results.

The voice of fear feels entirely different from the voice of love. It feels creepy and cold and leaves you unsettled and upset. It does not deliver ease, solace, or peace. Instead, it thrives on demand, threat, protection, defense, and manipulation. It does not take you where you want to go. It does not relieve stress, but intensifies it.

> The part that is listening to the Voice for God is calm, always at rest and wholly certain. It is really the only part there is. The other part is a wild illusion, frantic and distraught, but without reality of any kind. Try today not to listen to it. Try to identify with the part of your mind where stillness and peace reign forever. Try to hear God's Voice call to you lovingly, reminding you that your Creator has not forgotten His Son.
>
> — W-49.2

> If you will lay aside the ego's voice, however loudly it may seem to call; if you will not accept its petty gifts that give you nothing that you really want; if you will listen with an open mind, that has not told you what salvation is; then you will hear the mighty Voice of truth, quiet in power, strong in stillness, and completely certain in Its messages.
>
> — W-106.1

Discerning between the voices of love and fear is like listening to two different radio stations. One plays heavy, loud, annoying music. Another plays music that is soothing, uplifting, and healing. Since the radio stations are within you, you can choose which one you set your dial on and reap the results of the kind of music each station is broadcasting.

## The Tummy Test

I heard about a businessman who considers important decisions while he eats dinner. As he dines he imagines that he will take one path among several alternatives. If he gets indigestion after dinner, he knows that the path he is considering is the wrong one for him. If he digests and sleeps well, he knows this path is the right one.

Your body and your feelings are always telling you whether or not any particular decision or direction is aligned with your well-being. Your body and feelings speak louder than your thinking mind, where all of your problems live. If a plan makes you uptight or sick to think about or do, it's not the way to go. If an idea uplifts and energizes you to consider or do it, that's it. Trust your deep inner knowing.

Ultimately only the voice of love is your own. Everything else doesn't belong to you. Claim what is rightfully yours, and your choices will work out miraculously.

> Your healing Voice protects all things today, and so I leave all things to You. I need be anxious over nothing. For Your Voice will tell me what to do and where to go; to whom to speak and what to say to him, what thoughts to think, what words to give the world.
>
> — W-275.2:1-3

You have not been left in the cold to make sense of a senseless world. That is the ego's interpretation of life. The Holy Spirit within you recognizes that your every step is a part of your journey home. You can turn your back on love, but love cannot and will not turn its back on you. The Voice for God will always tell you what to do, if you ask sincerely. If your child came to you with an important question and you had the answer, you would not withhold it. Neither will your heavenly Parent withhold wisdom from you. Life is not a mystery, and the key to enlightenment is not hidden. Look for truth where it is, not where others have been looking for it or where you have been told it is. Everything you need to know is given freely, seeded within you. Seek not outside yourself.

> "Who walks with me?" This question should be asked a thousand times a day, till certainty has ended doubting and established peace. Today let doubting cease.
>
> — W-156.8:1-3

# 13

# A QUIET PATH IN SUMMER

When I lived on the island of Kauai, I often visited the pristine and magical beach at Hanalei Bay, where *South Pacific* was filmed. Every day at sunset a couple named Doug and Sandy would set up beach chairs and play soothing music on guitar and ukulele, to the delight of anyone who wished to show up and listen. You cannot imagine a more heavenly scene.

One day a listener asked Doug why he and his partner did not charge for their impromptu concerts. "We do it just because we love to," he answered. "We are happy to share our music with anyone who appreciates it." He went on, "One day a fellow came and asked, 'What is the most exciting dream you have for yourself?' I told him, 'I would love to have a custom-made guitar by a famous guitar maker on the Big Island of Hawaii.' The fellow replied, 'I so appreciate both of you coming here every sunset and blessing the community. I would like to get you that guitar.' He did. It cost $10,000."

While you and I have been taught that we must struggle for our good, *A Course in Miracles* teaches that struggle is not required, and we are provided for by grace.

One of the Course's most comforting passages, quoted in the Preface to this book, bears repeating here:

> When you have learned how to decide with God, all decisions become as easy and as right as breathing. There is no effort, and you will be led as gently as if you were being carried down a quiet path in summer.

> — T-14.IV.6:1-2

Let's look more deeply into the belief that we must fight our way to heaven, so we can dispel the illusion and replace it with a gentler path. To begin, we must set our intention to rise above the mass agreement that pain is the parent of peace. You have been taught that if you are not busting your butt, you are a slacker. "Success is 1 percent inspiration and 99 percent perspiration." "No pain, no gain." Yet if you observe people whose lives are steeped in anxious effort, you will see that there is no end to their quest for peace. There is always one more project to complete, one more hurdle to jump, one more enemy to defeat before joy is attainable. But joy is not the result of struggle. Joy is the result of choosing joy. You cannot get apples from orange seeds, and you cannot get peace from strife. *Belief* in hard makes the world hard. Transfer your allegiance to ease, and the world becomes far lighter.

## Beyond Contrast

Another illusion the world holds dear is that contrast is required to experience happiness. You have been told that you cannot have joy without sorrow, resolution without conflict, laughter without tears, love without hate, rest without work, healing without illness, release without bondage, forgiveness without guilt, and heaven without hell. Certainly we can learn through contrast and use differences to sharpen our awareness. But gross contrast serves only at the initial stage of the spiritual journey. If Advanced Intelligence cannot get your attention through subtle contrasts, it will use more blunt contrasts as educational tools. If you do not feel the nudge, you end up with a slap. Not because pain is God's will, but because nothing less will get your attention. It is not God's plan that makes life hard, but human resistance. There are ways to learn that do not require pain. As you elevate to more refined levels of experience, differences become subtler, softer, and barely perceptible, and drama gives way to a new kind of story without hardship.

In the world of polarity, everything exists in opposites that reinforce each other. The world to which ACIM invites us is one of unity. "The opposite of love is fear, but what is all-encompassing can have no opposite" (T-In.1:8). There is a light more constant than the sun that disappears at night—a life that lives without death, a love that surpasses brief conditional relationships, a self not subject to destruction by external forces, a reality not impinged upon by illusions.

> In Heaven . . . [e]verything is clear and bright, and calls forth one response. There is no darkness and there is no contrast . . . There is a sense of peace so deep that no dream in this world has ever brought even a dim imagining of what it is.
>
> — Excerpted from T-13.XI.3:7-13

## By Grace I Live

While many religions and spiritual paths focus on the importance of good works, they often overlook or underplay the presence and power of grace. Grace is the state of being in which we are loved unconditionally and all that we need is provided for us by the benevolent hand of God. You don't have to earn your good. It is given freely and generously. Well-being is not an achievement you earn. It is your birthright. Remove from your mind the belief that there is something you must do first before you can be happy. Safety, vitality, sustenance, and soul fulfillment are yours by virtue of your identity as the progeny of God. Love is *where* you are because love is *what* you are. Your blessings proceed from heaven without interruption.

I was coaching a client who recalled that many years ago she experienced a golden phase of her life in which everything flowed perfectly. The right people showed up, all of her decisions worked in her favor, and it seemed that she could do no wrong. "I just wish I could get back to that effortless way of living," she declared. Then she thought for a moment and made a very poignant statement: "Maybe everything has always gone right for me, and it still is, but I have just not been aware of it."

125

No truer words have ever been spoken. I told my client that if she could just step back into the consciousness of the golden presence in and around her, she would find that in truth she has never left the domain of blessing.

Even while you labor under the illusion that you must provide for yourself, God is caring for you. Consider the trillions of microscopic processes that keep your body alive and healthy. They are not under your conscious control. Your heart beats, your lungs breathe, your stomach digests, and all of your organs play their intricate and complex roles perfectly. Neither can you manage the vast brilliant systems mechanizing the universe around you. The earth maintains its perfect distance from the sun at its precise angle of tilt; water rises from the sea to rain on the plants that feed you, and it evaporates to perpetually repeat the cycle; a cut on your finger heals without you knowing how to regrow your skin. You participate in a supremely intelligent process far vaster than you can supervise. You may believe you are responsible for your well-being, but you are not. You are responsible to *cooperate,* not *control.* You can say with full confidence, "I am sustained by the Love of God" (W, Lesson 50).

We now arrive at the one Lesson that can relieve you of all of your burdens if you let it:

> By grace I live. By grace I am released.
>
> — W, Lesson 169

You can put aside any notion that you must *become* worthy. You are *already* worthy. I look back on the many foolish things I have done, the mistakes I have made, the unkindnesses I have shown myself and others, and all the reasons my ego tells me I must become a better person to deserve the things I want. Then I realize that even while I was asleep at the wheel of my life, a Higher Power was guiding and caring for me. This is a very humbling status to recognize. How I have been provided for, in spite of my stupors and errors, is a complete and total miracle. I cannot explain it except by the hand of grace, which holds us all. My life is a course in miracles, and so is yours.

## Grace in Action

Accepting grace does not mean that you simply lie in bed and wait for checks to float through your window. You were not born to be a passive observer of life. You were born to dive into the adventure and allow Higher Power to operate *through* you, as well as *for* you.

There are, of course, supernatural interventions in which angels appear and rescue people from car wrecks and other dangerous situations. Such phenomena are exciting and awe inspiring to behold. More often, grace flows to us through worldly avenues and actions we take.

The spiritual teacher Bashar tells of a woman who wanted to travel around the world and visit sacred sites, but she had no money. So she proposed to an airline that if the company would fly her around the world, she would take photographs for the airline's magazine. The airline agreed and gave her a round-the-world trip with first-class accommodations in exchange for her photos—plus they paid her.

I know another woman who loves movies, so she volunteered at the Sundance Film Festival. Through an uncanny series of events, she met Robert Redford and became his personal assistant.

As I have mentioned, my mentor Hilda Charlton never charged a penny for the many years of healing and teaching she generously gave. Grateful students gave her everything she needed, including a comfortable Manhattan apartment, vehicles, clothing, and health care. One day an appreciative student came to her apartment building and gave the doorman an envelope containing $5,000 for Hilda. This woman of faith knew she was sustained by God, and her good found its way to her, as it does to you and me.

## The Fire of Purpose

Choosing the path of ease does not mean that you get lazy, flee from challenges, or quit if your process grows difficult. It means that you ask Spirit to help you move beyond perceived obstacles. "I will step back and let Him lead the way" (W, Lesson 155). If there is something you need to know or do, you will be told. If you *burn with the fire of purpose*, you will recognize yourself to be greater than any challenge that confronts you and you will be specifically directed to the path most in harmony with your calling. Higher Power will provide the ways and means to achieve your goal without any stress on your part. Work may be required. Fear never is.

You don't have to buck your way to your good. Science and faith essayist Lyell Rader advised, "If you can't pray a door open, don't pry it open." What is right for you wants to come to you. What is not right for you wants to flee from you. If you have to fight to get or keep something, it doesn't belong to you and you are better off without it. Something better belongs to you. *Struggle to get, struggle to keep.* Things belong to you not by your manipulation, but by right of your consciousness. Hold your consciousness at the highest elevation you can, and what is yours will know your face.

Many people misinterpret Buddha as teaching that we should not desire. You cannot not desire. To be alive is to desire. The desire to have no desires is a desire. Buddha was telling us *to not be attached* to our desires. Even the Dalai Lama, considered by many to be the most enlightened Buddhist alive, has favorite toys and activities. But he plays with them rather than letting them control his happiness. As a boy he was fascinated with telescopes, and as an elder he watches television and laughs at the shows. He also laughs at the show called Earth. When you and I can laugh at what once seemed so serious, we have risen beyond fear and we are well on our way to enlightenment. ". . . every tear is wiped away in laughter and in love" (T-27.I.5:5).

You can shortcut years or lifetimes of hardship by accepting grace and letting ease be your guide. *A Course in Miracles* is a time collapser and a suffering reducer. You were not born to ricochet around Earth forever. If you are a stubborn do-it-yourselfer, you will keep fighting to make good things happen. Meanwhile, you have a potent Companion capable of providing for your every need. ". . . that one Voice appoints your function, and relays it to you, giving you the strength to understand it, do what it entails, and to succeed in everything you do that is related to it" (W-154.3:2).

> Who would attempt to fly with the tiny wings of a sparrow when the mighty power of an eagle has been given him?

> — M-4.I.2:2

# Why Is the Course Written in Patriarchal Language?

*A Course in Miracles* is written in the masculine gender only. God is referred to as "He," as is the Holy Spirit, and the offspring of God is called the "Son of God." We might wonder why the author did not take more care to honor women or embrace the feminine principle. If Jesus is truly one with the all-knowing Mind of God, did he miss the '60s? Is he unaware of the women's movement? Is Jesus a sexist?

A divine illuminated being whose love and compassion are universal would certainly not leave women out of salvation or demean their identity. There are several reasons ACIM is written in the masculine gender.

First, Jesus is teaching the singular nature of God rather than separateness. "He" and "She" represent a polarized universe in which creation is split into opposites. The Course seeks to restore our minds to wholeness rather than duality.

As for the "Son of God," there is one offspring of God—all of us—which is also not subject to division by gender. Spirit is neither male nor female. So Jesus chose to use a oneness term for all of us rather than twoness.

Human beings project human attributes onto God. Since we live in a largely patriarchal culture, God is usually related to as a "he." Since Jesus is speaking to us in terms we understand, represented largely by the Christian, Muslim, and Jewish religions, he is stepping into our current belief system to make the Course palatable to us.

I am certain that the author of *A Course in Miracles* would not object to God being called "She," or simply "Spirit," "Creator," "Higher Power," "Allah," "Jehovah," or whatever term brings us peace. We must each relate to God in the way that unites us with Him, Her, or It.

It would be a sad loss if some students of the Course put it aside because they feel offended by the masculine appellation. The life-changing benefits of the program span far beyond human gender. The Course is for all people, equally valuable and lovable to our Creator.

## 14

# THE DISTRACTOR FACTOR

In the Preface to this book, I mentioned that everyone who studies *A Course in Miracles* has resistance. If you had no resistance, you would not need to do the Course. If you had no resistance, you would not be in a body on Earth. You would have no fears, no upsets, and you would live in a state of constant bliss. If that is you, then you can skip this chapter. If, however, you still get irritated at anyone, or you miss any practice sessions of the ACIM Workbook Lessons, you will find great value in this chapter.

The Course anticipates our resistance and addresses it early in the Workbook and often thereafter. It knows we are going to do our utmost to distract ourselves from the truths in the Course that the ego does not want to face. What ego wants to hear that the world it has convinced you is so real is actually a sham of smoke and mirrors? And that your search for someone who will make you happy is really your search for yourself. And that money, pills, and social status have none of the power you have ascribed to them. What self-respecting ego would not rear back and pull every trick, tool, and weapon it could muster from its arsenal in order to keep you engaged in the world it has created? Do not underestimate the ego's resourcefulness in holding you captive in the castle of illusion that fear has built—even if your escape would remove you from hell and plant your feet in heaven.

Rather than deny our resistance or try to distract ourselves further, we must address resistance head-on and look for strong yet graceful ways to move beyond it. Fortunately, because the Holy Spirit is smarter than the ego, there are ways to surmount the wall of flak that the armies of the night have launched to shroud the coming dawn.

## Resistance Busters

### 1. Do the Workbook Lessons.

When students tell me, "I started to study the Course, but I didn't understand it and I stopped," I ask them, "Have you done the Workbook Lessons?"

"No, I started with the Text and couldn't get through it. That's when I put it aside."

"Forget about the Text for the moment and start with the Workbook Lessons," I tell them. "Then you can return to the Text, and it will be easier to understand."

The Course gives us clues to overcome resistance before we even open Workbook Lesson 1:

> Some of the ideas the workbook presents you will find hard to believe, and others may seem to be quite startling. This does not matter. You are merely asked to apply the ideas as you are directed to do. You are not asked to judge them at all. You are asked only to use them. It is their use that will give them meaning to you, and will show you that they are true.
>
> Remember only this; you need not believe the ideas, you need not accept them, and you need not even welcome them. Some of them you may actively resist. None of this will matter, or decrease their efficacy. But do not allow yourself to make exceptions in applying the ideas the workbook contains, and whatever your reactions to the ideas may be, use them. Nothing more than that is required.
>
> — W-In.8-9

So just keep going with the Lessons. Don't stop. Some of the Lessons will resonate with you and others will not. If you don't understand some of the Lessons, do them anyway. If you don't like them, do them anyway. If you miss some practice periods, keep going. If you miss a day of doing the Lessons, continue the next day. If you miss a week of doing the Lessons, start again. Don't use any excuse to stop. Staying with the Lessons will save your life spiritually and could save it physically. The Lessons work if you work them.

No matter how many Lessons or exercise periods you miss, do not use your lapses as an excuse to feel guilty or beat yourself up. That is exactly what the ego wants you to do. The goal of the Course is to end guilt. So if you miss some Lessons or exercises and you choose inner peace anyway, you are in a roundabout way mastering the Course.

Yet the Lessons are extremely important to keep up with, so do not use the instruction above to justify delay. The Course tells us, "Delay does not matter in eternity, but it is tragic in time" (T-5.VI.1:3).

Do each Workbook Lesson as soon as possible after you awaken in the morning—*before* you check your e-mail, Facebook, or voice mail; watch the news; start work; or get involved in the activities of the day. Do not wait until you have a convenient moment to practice. Convenience is not something that happens to you. It is something you choose. If you let the day encroach before you connect with God, you will relegate God to second (or third or fourth or fifth or last) place in your life. *Your spiritual connection is more important than anything else you do.* If there is something you absolutely have to do first, like get the kids off to school, do it. But return to your Lesson as soon as you can.

As you practice the Lessons, your resistance will gradually drop away and the program will become an ecstatic celebration. The magnificent truths upon which the Course is built will become real in your life, and you will experience healing. ACIM becomes only lighter and more fun; the most challenging Lessons become your best friends. Resistance is simply a speed bump you must drive over on the way to the party. But the party goes on, and you are on the guest list.

**2. Study the Text in the way and order you feel guided.**

*A Course in Miracles* is holographic. Every sentence contains the essence of the whole. With the exception of the Workbook Lessons, the material is not necessarily linear. Some people believe they need to read the Text word for word, cover to cover, beginning to end. If you feel so guided, that will work. But you can also study the Text and Manual for Teachers in any order you are guided. I recommend that you read all of it, for there are jewels to be mined in every sentence. *How* you do that is up to you.

Feel free to go to different sections of the Text and Manual for Teachers as they call to you. Or just open to any page and get the message you need to hear. The Holy Spirit will speak to you through whatever words you are reading. If you are open and ready, you will be enlightened by the briefest phrase. The Text, although apparently intellectual, runs far deeper than the mind. When you study ACIM, you are immersing your mind in *a consciousness*, not just information. The goal of the Course is to attain a state of awareness. Studying the Text will take you there as you feel guided.

**3. Soothe your resistance.**

Another way to handle the resistant ego is to soothe it. What would you say to a child who is afraid? Would you shame him, beat him, and force him to do what scares him? Or would you kneel to meet him face to face, hold his hands, look him in the eyes, ask him what he is afraid of, and help him understand that he is bigger than his fear? Kindness heals, and dealing with the ego is not an exception to this principle.

The ego believes its job is to protect you from threats. It is determined to fulfill its perceived role, because it believes its life and yours depend on it. If you confront your ego head on and try to crack it, overpower it, deny it, fight it, demean it, or diminish it, it will not just agree with you and go away. ". . . you cannot escape from the ego by humbling it or controlling it or punishing it" (T-4. VI.3:8). Under perceived attack, it will do what any red-blooded ego would do: marshal its defenses, puff itself up, and fight harder than ever.

Tell your ego that you mean it no harm and it can continue to do its job, which it holds so dear. Assuage it by letting it know that your intention is to help it fight less and relax more. Assure it that you are not threatening it. You just have something else you need to do for the moment (your Workbook Lesson, meditation, prayer, or any other activity in which you immerse yourself in a higher reality). For example, when I guide a group meditation, I tell the students, "Let's just put the cares of the day aside for a few minutes. If you want to take them back after that time, you can. But for now we will simply focus on peace."

To the ego, this is very comforting. If you were an ego, you would probably think, *I guess I can stand a few minutes without having to struggle. I can take up my job after that time.*

This approach may sound infantile, but remember that you are dealing with an entity that is simultaneously brilliant in its capacity to devise complex schemes and infantile in its need to fight for its survival.

Honor your ego by appreciating the job it is doing for you. Your ego marks the identity of the vessel that carries you across the sea of life. It helps you discern your unique vantage point in the universe. As a survival mechanism, it works. It keeps you on the proper side of the road when driving and a safe distance from steep cliffs. So thank your ego for all of its efforts to keep you alive and focused on your human journey. Appreciating your ego will make you and it feel better and clear the pathway to move beyond it.

If you work with the ego gently and gradually, rather than coming at it with a battering ram and trying to annihilate it, you will gain far more ground than making war on it. When you make war on your ego, it has already won, because it defines itself in terms of war. If you enfold the ego with love, you rise above it and master the resistance it offers. When love and fear meet, only love remains.

**4. Notice when and how resistance arises and the form it takes.**

Much of the world's activity is an attempt to escape from fear. Indeed it is our purpose to escape from fear. But *how* you escape from fear makes all the difference in whether or not you succeed.

You can push fear to the side by substituting one distraction for another, which is not escape at all. Or you can escape into truth, which yields true freedom.

Many habits and addictions are forms of resistance, bunkers *apparently* safe from pain, but *effectively* safe from love. Here are some of the ways we numb ourselves from pain: constantly working, endlessly striving to prove ourselves, terminal busyness, anxious eating, alcoholism, drugging, shopping, compulsive sex, sugar and adrenaline rushes, hypnotized television watching or computer engagement, constant texting, nonstop talking, obsessive cleaning, hyper-analysis, gossip, fighting, and drama. One of the most illuminating exercises I have ever conducted in a seminar was to ask each participant to answer the question, "How do you medicate your pain?" The students stated the examples above and more. This was not a seminar for addicts, criminals, or mental patients. These were healthy, well-functioning, productive members of society. Meanwhile, they all bore sufficient pain in their lives that they needed to immerse themselves in one illusion or another to take the edge off of their discomfort.

The first step to overcoming resistance is to *recognize your resistant behavior.* No unconscious behavior can long stand in the light of higher awareness. Notice, for example, when you open the refrigerator door to grab a snack when you are not hungry. "This is anxious eating," you can say to yourself. In that moment, do not judge yourself or fight the behavior. Just notice it. Or, "I just got into a petty argument over money." Or, "I just sat here with people I love and spent half my time texting." Identify with the *witness* rather than the *doer.* The more you gain perspective, the more leverage you will find to make healthy choices. Beating yourself up for unwanted behaviors never works. Guilt does not stop the pain that causes addiction. It perpetuates it. Inner peace is your strongest ally in any campaign to improve your life.

Next, notice the results of your resistant behavior. Is it really getting you what you want? The second piece of pie tastes good for a moment, but the next time you step on the scale or look in the mirror, what it costs outweighs what you have gained (okay, pun intended). Watching mindless television for hours every evening may help you forget the troubles of your day, but do you really feel better afterward? Does having sex without a heart connection really fulfill you? Dessert, television, and sex serve their purpose, but when they become substitutes for connection to self and others, they divert you from the happiness you seek.

Use the same technique when facing resistance to *A Course in Miracles*. At first simply notice the resistance. Become aware of the things your ego tells you to do that prevent you from studying or applying the Course. The e-mails you must answer, the people you must contact, the errands you must run, the things you must fix, and the emergencies you must respond to rather than doing today's Lesson . . . and on and on. Without judgment or resistance, shine light on the ways you distract yourself from experiencing inner peace. Awareness is the beginning of healing. After a while your resistance will lose its power to distract you and you will be in a better position to make decisions that truly serve you, such as mastering *A Course in Miracles*.

### 5. Cultivate habits that truly make you feel good.

When you try to get rid of something, you focus energy on the unwanted behavior, which feeds and expands it. Instead, substitute another activity that works better. Once again, think of your consciousness as a radio that is always tuned to one station or another. If you don't like the station your radio is tuned to, yelling at that station or banging the radio will not stop it. You will do better to simply switch your tuner to a station you prefer.

A student told me, "I've been smoking pot every day for ten years. I have tried to quit many times, but nothing has worked."

I told her, "Then don't try to quit."

She looked surprised.

"What activities do you do that make you feel better than smoking pot?" I asked.

"I like doing yoga, meditating, and coming to your classes."

"Then focus on doing yoga, meditating, and attending the classes," I told her. "Forget about the pot habit for the moment and give your attention to higher-frequency activities. Then the denser habits will drop away naturally."

When I saw this woman a few months later, she told me, "Your advice worked. I felt so good doing the things I love that I lost interest in pot. I haven't smoked in a long time."

When you cultivate activities that truly bring you joy, you establish yourself in the domain of the soul. Notice how good you feel when you tap into the peace and release ACIM offers. Letting go of upset feels a lot better than holding on to it. Seeing the Christ in your brother feels a lot better than regarding him as the devil. Being gentle with yourself feels a lot better than beating yourself up. Just keep doing what makes you feel best, and what is less than best will gradually disappear from your experience.

## Don't Believe Everything You Think

When I was a guest on a radio show geared to transformational topics, a caller asked, "Why is there so much road rage?"

The host answered, "Because people want to be angry, and traffic is a convenient excuse."

The host's answer was a perfect illustration of the ACIM Lesson, "I am never upset for the reason I think" (W, Lesson 5). We choose upset because we find it more attractive than peace. Events don't make us upset. We make ourselves upset and then designate events as the cause. We could just as easily—far *more* easily—choose peace. "I choose the joy of God instead of pain" (W, Lesson 190).

When I presented a residential seminar at a rustic retreat center, a participant I'll call Barbara had lots of complaints: "My room doesn't have enough ventilation . . . My bed is too small . . . I don't like my roommate . . ." and so on. By the end of the retreat, I wondered if perhaps I had chosen the wrong facility and I should use a higher-end hotel.

After the retreat, Barbara went with another participant to spend several days at a luxury resort on Maui's exclusive south shore—at $500 a night. Later I spoke with the woman who had accompanied Barbara. "How did you like the resort?" I asked.

"I loved it," she replied. "But my roommate complained the whole time. She found a million things wrong with it."

Barbara took her consciousness with her wherever she went. The rustic retreat was not good enough, and the luxury resort was not good enough. She was seeing the entire world through the lens of "not good enough."

Upset is a lens we choose to filter experiences. You participate in what disturbs you. The ego's world is built on grievances, so it can and will use every little thing it sees as grounds for grievance. It believes that whining is winning, while you are really losing. The Spiritual Eye sees through a different lens. It sees everything as grounds for gratitude, the shortest route to success and fulfillment.

Resistance is not something that happens to you. It is something you choose because you believe you receive value from it. When the value you perceive in wellness exceeds the value you perceive in upset, inner peace shall be yours.

## Keep the Change

The ego takes refuge in familiarity and is threatened by change. It defines the known as preferable to the unknown, even if the known sucks. This is one reason why so many people stay in abusive relationships. The relationship, although painful, is at least predictable. The ego equates predictability with safety, even if the predictable is disaster. To the Holy Spirit, Who values inner peace more than injury, this thought system is insane. But so is the ego's entire delusional thought system.

The ego actively resists any attempt to alter the world it has created. What the ego does not tell you is that the world it has created is killing you. When something comes along that threatens the ego's world, it will do *anything it can* to keep you from stepping ahead to freedom. Often the bigger the change for the better, the bigger the emergency, drama, or setback the ego manufactures. But the ego cannot stop you unless you let it. Just keep going in spite of the ego's attempts to sabotage your progress, and you will triumph. An Arab proverb says, "The dogs bark, but the caravan moves on."

The Holy Spirit regards change in an entirely different way. It welcomes, celebrates, and makes positive use of change. The Manual for Teachers tells us, "It takes great learning to understand that all things, events, encounters and circumstances are helpful" (M-4.I.A.4:5); and ". . . trust remains the bedrock of the teacher of God's whole thought system" (M-4.III.1:6). The Text affirms, ". . . trust would settle every problem now" (T-26.VIII.2:3). When a friend of mine was going through a divorce, he took a bunch of papers and wrote "TRUST" in big letters on each page. Then he spread the pages out on the floor and lay down on them, symbolically immersing himself in a field of trust. His divorce settled amicably, and eventually he remarried and began a lovely family, with which he is now very happy. Define all change as good, even if you don't see the blessing at the moment. It is there and will reveal itself. Indian poet Rabindranath Tagore said, "Faith is the bird that feels the light and sings when the dawn is still dark."

We are all masters of distraction. We are adept at making simple things complicated and making right things wrong. The world is a massive sleight of hand, confounding reality with appearances and rendering pain more attractive than peace. Doublespeak is accepted as a substitute for communication, and we believe we gain at the loss of another. We flee from light and hide in darkness. We believe the real part of us is fake, and the fake part of us is real. We believe that if others knew the truth about us, they would run away screaming, while if they actually knew the truth about us, they would love us forever. We have tricked ourselves into incredible smallness.

Yet the taste of freedom has touched your lips, and you have begun to suspect that the way you have been told life works is not so. Fingers of light have begun to pierce the dungeon walls that once seemed impenetrable. You are starting to recognize that you deserve better. You know too much to turn back now. You may doze for moments here and there, but you cannot sleep as deeply as you once did. Your resistance is dissolving, and you are more interested in getting on with the journey than in clinging to a rock that once seemed safe but now drags you down. The trinkets of childhood have lost their glitter.

Work the Lessons. Not just those in the ACIM Workbook, but all the life lessons that come to you. The people, events, and experiences that show up in your world are not random. They are orchestrated by a Higher Power that loves you in ways you do not understand. At every moment God is extending a hand to you to lift you out of quicksand and onto higher ground. Stop fighting life and let it love you. Miracles are seeking you. Now you must let them find you.

Leave room for Him, and you will find yourself so filled with power that nothing will prevail against your peace.

— T-14.XI.15:5

# 15

# TIMELESS
# LOVE

What would you do if you had more time? What would you do
if you had less time? What would you do if you had no time? How
would your life be different if time were not a factor?

For most people, time is a problem because we believe we don't
have enough of it. We regard time as our enemy, ticking away
precious minutes of life. People get stressed over time, fight over it,
complain about it ("I gave you the best years of my life!"), and pay
for services by the hour. Things we cherish come to an end. People
we love die. Time, invisible yet apparently rock solid, exerts silent
dominion over our lives.

*A Course in Miracles* views time in a very different light. It tells
us that our true Self lives far beyond time, and "the purpose of
time is to enable you to learn how to use time constructively"
(T-1.I.15:2). We are here to employ time in our favor rather than
let it crush us. Time helps us focus and discover the difference
between the minutes that bring us joy and those that bring us
sorrow. What is the purpose of a day? Is it to work to earn money
and flit about on endless errands? Or is it to savor connection, express creativity, and celebrate blessings? ACIM suggests, "Each day
should be devoted to miracles" (T-1.I.15:1). If you have ever had
a miraculous day in which everything unfolded effortlessly, you
have experienced the true purpose of a day, to which you have a
right *every day.*

Time further urges us to make the most of the space between
when we arrive in the world and when we depart. If you were to
leave this world now, would you be satisfied with how you have
spent your time? If not, what would make your remaining time

here more meaningful? Likewise, at the end of each day conduct an honest introspection about what you did with your time today. What would you do differently tomorrow to make your precious time count?

*We ask for long life, but 'tis deep life, or grand moments, that signify. Let the measure of time be spiritual, not mechanical.*

— RALPH WALDO EMERSON

## Lovers Make a Fool of Time

ACIM suggests that time is a story we made up, a game we have agreed to play. An invention of the intellect, time expands or contracts according to the consciousness you hold at any given moment. It is more like rubber than concrete. When you feel fearful, rushed, stressed, or upset, you experience less time. When you are relaxed and in the flow of life, you experience more time. When you are completely in the moment, you do not experience time at all. As you step into joy, you escape the domain time appears to rule.

It is said that "lovers make a fool of time." When you are in love, you care not about time. All you want to do is enjoy being with your beloved. Who cares what the clock says? When you are in fear, every second ticks by painfully slowly and the watched pot never boils. So the secret to triumph over the tyranny of time is to stay in love. Not simply romantic love, but the awareness that love is everywhere and you are in its midst. To immerse yourself in such an expansive consciousness, drink in the ecstatic poetry of God-intoxicants like Rumi, Hafiz, and Kabir.

Indigenous people have a very different sense of time from those of us in more mechanized civilizations. People close to the earth live in the here and now. Time is a largely irrelevant factor in their lives. When I lived in Fiji, a native fellow served as caretaker for our property. I once said to him, "Maybe one day we will build a rock wall over there." Then he asked me, "You want me to do that now?" The "maybe one day" part of my sentence did not register in his mind, because the only day he was aware of was the one we were in. He didn't have a concept of the future. His only concept was the now. The Fijians do not know the dates of their own birthdays or those of their children. What does it matter? If it is not now, it is not.

> How can a world of time and place exist, if you remain as God created you?

> — W-132.9:4

## Ready Now

ACIM invites us to step out of time into eternity. Eternity is not a realm you enter after you die. It is an expanded reality that exists now. Now is the closest approximation in time to the experience of eternity. You cannot get to eternity through time. There is no progression of Thursday, Friday, Saturday . . . eternity. Eternity does not start when time ends. It is already here, welcoming us to enter when we are ready.

> Why wait for Heaven? It is here today. Time is the great illusion it is past or in the future. Yet this cannot be, if it is where God wills His Son to be. How could the Will of God be in the past, or yet to happen? What He wills is now . . .

> — W-131.6:1-6

Religions teach that you may attain heaven one day if you become good enough. ACIM assures that you have a right to enter heaven now because you are *already* good enough. Jesus taught, "The kingdom of heaven is within you" (Luke 17:21); "Come, for all things are now ready" (Luke 14:17); and "Do you not say, 'There are yet four months, then comes the harvest'? Look, I tell you, lift up your eyes, and see that the fields are white for harvest" (John 4:35). You can evaluate the truth in a religion or any spiritual path by the size of the gap it defines between you and the heaven you deserve. The greater the gap, the farther the religion has drifted from truth. The smaller the gap, the closer to truth. When there is no gap, you are home.

## How the Ego and Spirit Each Use Time

The ego uses time as a tactic to delay the experience of oneness. Novelist Ray Cummings said that time is "what keeps everything from happening at once." Everything that has ever existed, does exist, will exist, and could exist, exists now. The universe is holographic. The whole is contained in every part. Everything is here and now. The ego invented time to push away what is already now, as it uses space to distance us from what is already here. In the realm of Spirit, the separations defined by time and space do not exist. Without the ego's divisions of time and space, we would have everything we want here and now. We would *be* everything we want here and now. Then there would be no wanting or waiting, because in such a consciousness we have *become* what we desire.

The master reframer Holy Spirit is not thwarted by the ego's use of time as a separating device. Higher Awareness spins the illusion of time in our favor by redefining time as a focusing aid. When we use time to discover, enjoy, and express the holiness of life, it becomes our friend. When you engage in activities meaningful to your soul, you feel filled. Time becomes an asset when you place it on the altar of healing rather than chasing it or running from it. The word *deadline* is an apt description of how the ego uses time to frighten you into submission. By contrast, the Holy Spirit throws you only lifelines. To the ego, time is a relentless taskmaster. To the Spirit, time is our friend, calling us to receive the gift every moment offers.

> If you achieve the faintest glimmering of what love means today, you have advanced in distance without measure and in time beyond the count of years to your release.
>
> — W-127.7:1

## No Fear in the Now

All fear is of future events. If you are established in the now moment, you cannot be afraid. You can experience reality only now. Since love is the only reality, the only time to find love is now. All other uses of time are distortions that will drive you crazy if you indulge them.

While I was walking on a forest path, I looked down to see that I was about to step on a rattlesnake. Quickly I jumped back. The rattlesnake, no happier to see me than I was to see it, slithered into a bush. When I thought about how close I had come to being injured, a chill of fear rippled through me. But in the moment of seeing the snake and stepping back, there was no fear. I instinctively knew what I had to do and I did it. Only when the mind interceded did fear arise. This experience taught me that fear is never necessary. If you are in a threatening situation, you will know what to do and you will do it. Psychological threat is far more menacing than physical threat because it drags you into a mire of angst that has nothing to do with what is happening at the moment. Should you feel fear, ask yourself, "Am I okay here and now?" Nearly every time, your answer will be "yes." If you are not okay here and now, ask yourself, "What do I need to do in this moment to handle the situation without letting fear run the show?" Fear and drama are not required or helpful. Trust and connection to Source are your best allies to navigate any situation.

If you feel afraid, just let the feeling be and observe it. Identify with the onlooker standing apart from the fear rather than the one who is afraid. Don't pile stress upon stress or judge yourself as a failure if you experience fear. It comes with the human experience. But there is more to you than the human experience. Divine experience is your birthright and destiny. Establish yourself in the now, and fear will lose its power over your life.

## Portals to Eternity

While you remain in time, make it your friend. Live by *kairos*, the Greek word for "in God's right timing," rather than by *chronos*, the seconds, minutes, and hours your watch ticks away. *Timing* is more important than time, and no matter how much or how little time you have, you always have timing.

A heavenly moment, even while you walk the earth, is a portal to eternity. Each day seek and find as many portals to eternity as you can. Any moment in which you feel peace or joy is a portal to eternity, because the hallmark of eternity is well-being. You can easily enter parallel realities with a slight dimensional shift. The key is to choose your reality *consciously* rather than waiting or hoping for your good to come to you. Go to the place in consciousness where the success you seek is *already* accomplished, and you will hasten its demonstration in time. All the good you seek is already here. It's not about time. It's about timelessness.

> If you would remember eternity, you must look only on the eternal.
>
> — T-10.V.14:5

# 16

# HEALTHY, WEALTHY, AND WISE

"Several years ago I was diagnosed with AIDS, cancer, and leukemia," a young man at one of my seminars reported. "I was not surprised. A year before that, my lover was killed in an auto accident. I remember telling people that without him I did not think I could go on living. Faced with such a diagnosis, I realized that I stood at the crossroads of life and death. I went into deep prayer and contemplation, and decided that I truly wanted to live. I chose to release my anger toward my partner for leaving, and toward the world for taking him. I was ready to move on to new purpose and meaning for my life."

The audience was perfectly still, everyone listening intently to this man's account.

He took a breath and added, "I just came from seeing my doctor, who found no trace of any of those diseases in my body. He gave me a clean bill of health."

Some people believe that because *A Course in Miracles* so consistently emphasizes the importance of the spirit and deemphasizes the importance of the body, it does not care whether or not you are healthy, and neither should you. *It is not so.* The Course wants you to enjoy vitality and wellness on every level: physically, emotionally, mentally, and spiritually. It finds no value in illness and does not ask you to endure pain. It does not call you to renounce your body or deny, demean, starve, or sacrifice it. To the contrary, ACIM wants you to keep your body in healthy, productive condition so you can feel good, be a vessel through which

Spirit expresses in the world, and let others see the light shining through you.

How, then, do we create and enjoy this level of well-being? Workbook Lesson 135 spells this out clearly. It says of the body:

> It needs no complicated structures of defense, no health-inducing medicine, no care and no concern at all . . . It will be strong and healthy if the mind does not abuse it by assigning it to roles it cannot fill . . . The body . . . becomes a healthy, serviceable instrument through which the mind can operate . . . In this capacity is health assured. For everything the mind employs for [helping in a plan which far exceeds its own protection] will function flawlessly, and with the strength that has been given it and cannot fail.

> — Excerpted from W, Lesson 135

Well-being, not illness, is the will of God. Get over any belief that you deserve or must put up with poor health. Do not use pain or sickness as a justification for self-punishment while you ascribe to God the role of punisher. God has never made anyone sick. We make ourselves sick by thinking, feeling, and acting out of harmony with our true nature. We gain health by aligning with Spirit's will for us, which is only love.

> Health is the result of relinquishing all attempts to use the body lovelessly.

> — T-8.VIII.9:9

## The Body as a Communication Device

The Course tells us that the only purpose of the body is to magnify the presence of love in the world. When you are healthy and happy, your body reflects wellness characteristic of heaven. Yet it is not the body itself that gives entrée to the holy place. It is your spirit. But in a world where people believe in bodies, the body can be used to point beyond itself.

Your body also shows you where you are in alignment with the flow of well-being, and where you have stepped out of alignment. Illness is an indication that there is a blockage in the current of life force. By the time you experience an illness, the blockage has already occurred on a mental and emotional level. Your body is not the cause of your mind and emotions; it is their effect. Illness is a wake-up call to recognize where the flow has been obstructed and, more important, to discover what attitudinal and/or lifestyle changes are required to restore it. When your body is in alignment with Spirit, universal law will keep you well.

No adverse physical condition need be permanent. There is no disease that always leads to the same results. Each person experiences results according to his or her consciousness. Many people have been healed of every disease. When you shift the consciousness that brought about an illness, its cause is gone, along with its effects. As mentioned earlier, your body is more liquid than solid, physically and metaphysically, constantly re-creating itself according to the current stream of consciousness you are holding. When that stream changes, so does the body.

Genuine healing goes far beyond the condition of the body. People who have a disability can be compelling teachers that their spirit is more real than their body. While their physical capacities seem limited, their souls are shining. Let us be grateful to those who radiate the presence of love and life in spite of apparent limitation. They are teachers of God. May we all rise beyond limitation of any kind. May our bodies and minds reflect the light that we are. May we all enjoy the healing and wellness we deserve as children of God.

## The Secret of Healing

Jesus Christ, like all agents of transformation, was able to achieve healing because his vision of his patients' wholeness was more powerful than their belief in disease. He understood that illness is the result of erroneous thinking, not a hard fact at all. If Jesus attributed reality or power to sickness and death, he could not have healed the sick and raised the dead. ("Only those who see the invisible can do the impossible.") Jesus's consciousness was so rooted in the invulnerability of Spirit that those around him were lifted to the expansive realm in which he dwelled. When they attained resonance with that frequency, they were healed.

Many of Jesus's statements as recorded in the New Testament affirm the principles of miracles as set forth in ACIM:

- When your eye is single, your whole body shall be filled with light (Luke 11:34).

- Therefore be perfect, as your heavenly Father is perfect (Matthew 5:48).

- You are the light of the world. A city on a hill cannot be hidden (Matthew 5:14).

Healing is the result of a shift in consciousness from separation to wholeness, a return to your true Self. I know of a woman who had vision problems for many years. She went to a healer who told her to see all things as perfect. She practiced the vision of perfection, and her vision problems completely disappeared. Her physical vision became a match to her spiritual vision.

I also know a couple whose daughter was born with a clubfoot, one foot turned at a right angle to the other. After repeated examinations and x-rays, doctors told Jessica's parents that she would need a series of surgeries and braces until she was six years old. Before Jessica's first surgery, her aunt met a Guatemalan healer on an airplane. She invited the fellow to a party at Jessica's house, where he prayed for a minute over the baby's foot. When the parents took the child for pre-op x-rays, the doctors were astonished. They said there was no problem at all with the foot. It had been entirely corrected. Jessica grew up to live a happy, healthy life.

Many healers have walked the earth, and many dwell among us now. They wear different costumes, speak different languages, and follow different traditions. Yet the principles that create healing are universal: *See perfection where others see limits. See wholeness where others see brokenness. Love while others fear.* That's the formula. All other details and instructions are given as you need them.

## All Is Yours Forever

Both health and wealth are signs and symbols that we live in an abundant universe, whose infinite resources are yours. In this sense, *A Course in Miracles* is the ultimate prosperity manual. The Course is uncompromising in its affirmation of your right to all the riches and wellness in the universe. It identifies you as heir to all that your heavenly Father is and owns. It sparks each of us to remember, "And so all things are given unto me forever and forever . . . I cannot lose, for I can only give, and everything is mine eternally" (W-343.1:7,11).

Unlike many prosperity courses, ACIM does not tell you how to get stuff. It teaches you how to get peace. Money is not the only measure of wealth, and possessions do not equal happiness. Only happiness equals happiness. Yet God's blessings manifest on Earth as they do in heaven. When you are established in soul serenity, you are in the perfect position to attract all you need, supplied by grace. "Surely goodness and mercy shall follow me all the days of my life . . ." (Psalm 23:6).

I was co-presenting a seminar with Neale Donald Walsch, author of the popular *Conversations with God* series. A participant asked Neale to give him a technique to help him manifest a car. Neale answered, "That would be more appropriate for an introductory workshop. This seminar doesn't teach you how to get a car. It teaches you how live in the consciousness of the divine."

Neale was not trying to dissuade the fellow from having his car. He was urging him to keep his priorities in order, to *create from the inside out.* When you dwell in a wealth mentality, you will have a car and all else you need without struggle or strain. The *experience* of wealth, not stuff, makes you rich. Most people believe, "If I can get the car, I will feel wealthy." That may be so. Yet universal abundance principles operate at a far deeper level: If you can realize how rich you already are, the car will show up as a manifestation of your wealth mentality. Like love, there are no external prerequisites to the experience of wealth. All the riches you could ever desire already exist right where you stand. "Remember that you are deprived of nothing . . ." (T-4.IV.3:3).

## When a Little Becomes a Lot

Film historian Katherine Orrison recounts a touching incident that occurred during the filming of *The Ten Commandments*. Iconic director Cecil B. DeMille was famous for meticulously setting up every scene of his movies before shooting began. Like the Ten Commandments tablets, DeMille's scripts were written in stone. One exception occurred while the crew was shooting in the Egyptian desert, where DeMille encountered a tribe of Bedouins. A woman in the tribe offered him and his crew all of the little the Bedouins had. DeMille was so impressed by her humble generosity that he inserted a new line into the movie. When Moses has been cast out of Egypt and he meets the sheepherder Sephora, she tells Moses, "We can offer you little, but we offer all we have." Moses, who had been privy to the opulence of Egypt as the Pharaoh's adopted son, was so moved by the wealth of spirit she displayed that he asked her to be his wife.

Real generosity is generosity of the spirit. It is the feeling that you are blessed with enough of all good things, and you are happy to bless others with your overflow. "My cup runneth over" (Psalm 23:5). I coach people who say they want to help others, but they are concerned that they have little or no money to do so. I tell them that there are an infinite number of ways to give without money. You can give time, talent, attention, listening, compassion, service, space, wisdom, or skill. Money is just one venue for support. Giving of the spirit is the richest way to give.

When you know you have enough for yourself, you know you have enough to give. To know that you *have* enough, you must know that you *are* enough. ACIM repeatedly reminds us that the greatest wealth is to remember our spiritual identity. "Now would I be as God created me" (W, Lesson 237).

## Gifts of the World and Gifts of God

You can distinguish between the gifts of the world and the gifts of God by one simple test: When you give a gift of the world, you have less and someone else has more. When you give a gift of God, both giver and receiver gain. The gifts of the world are physical commodities. The gifts of God are energetic experiences.

When you give love, kindness, patience, or forgiveness, you gain the experience of the gift you are giving, in the moment you give it, so you are as blessed as the receiver. The only gifts worth giving, ACIM tells us, are the gifts of God, which expand as you share them. "I will be healed as I let Him teach me to heal" (T-2.V.A.18:6).

## Your Golden Treasure-House

You were born to thrive, not just survive. Vibrant health and abundant wealth are your natural state. Dysfunction and deficiency, common as they appear, are the anomalies. ACIM calls us to purify our understanding of the will of God, which is always joy and never pain; always supply and never lack. The Course urges us to place our faith in God's ability to give, more than our willingness to accept. Grace is our natural state. Poverty and illness have no place in heaven, and they have no place on Earth as God intended it. The fact that these conditions exist is not a result of God's withholding. They spring from man's ignorance or rejection of wellness as our birthright. As we change our minds and accept the gifts given us, our storehouses shall be filled, and we shall return to the royal status from which we sprang and for which we are destined.

> This is the Holy Spirit's single gift; the treasure house to which you can appeal with perfect certainty for all the things that can contribute to your happiness. All are laid here already. All can be received but for the asking. Here the door is never locked, and no one is denied his least request or his most urgent need. There is no sickness not already healed, no lack unsatisfied, no need unmet within this golden treasury of Christ.
>
> — W-159.6:1-5

# Why Don't I Understand the Text?

You don't have to understand the Text. If you understood the Text, you would not need to study it. If you do not understand the Course with your intellect, you have not missed anything. It is said that "understanding is the booby prize." Do not allow lack of intellectual understanding to stop you from completing the Course. All the understanding you need will be given you precisely when it will serve you best.

What the ego "understands" is largely illusion. "I do not understand anything I see . . ." (W, Lesson 3). It is to the realm of the soul that *A Course in Miracles* calls us. The Text will heal you before you understand it. ACIM communicates more at the level of the heart than the mind. The intellectual concepts are the candy to keep your mind occupied while the Course transforms you.

*A Course in Miracles* is imbued with the power of Christ. Jesus has instilled healing energy in every word and sentence. When you read the Text, you are receiving ideas, some of which you will grasp. But more important, you are receiving peace, all of which you will recognize. I have often read sentences or passages in the Text that I did not understand at all. Yet when I finished, I felt deeply healed and soul nourished.

Read the Text and get what you can intellectually. Meanwhile practice the Workbook Lessons; they will bring the Text's principles to life. Above all else, let your heart absorb the essence spiritually. The heart and the intellect speak different languages, both of which have substance and value in their respective domains. The language of love is closer to your true nature than that of the mind. If you gain wisdom from the Course, you have gleaned a great gift. If you find love through the Course, you have found yourself.

# 17

# THE DREAMER AND THE DREAMED

Imagine that in a dream you are being chased by a bear. In another dream you are being chased by a hundred bears. In which situation are you in greater danger?

Before you answer, consider the first principle of miracles:

There is no order of difficulty in miracles.

— T-1.I.1:1

There is no order of difficulty in miracles because all of the conditions from which we desire for miracles to extricate us are equally illusory. They are all bad dreams, fictitious stories we have fabricated with our thoughts. You do not defeat dream monsters by battling them; that only reinforces their apparent reality. The most effective way to make a dream bear disappear is to wake up. To assign levels of difficulty to miracles is to give unmerited power to the challenges we perceive. In the Mind of God there are no degrees, hierarchies, gradations, competitions, or conflict. There is only oneness.

The answer to the question of whether you are in greater danger being chased by one dream bear or by a hundred, then, is that you are not in danger in either case. No matter how many bears *seem* to be chasing you, none of them can hurt you because they are all dream bears. Many dream bears are no more real than one dream bear, and they have no more power. Your safety lies not in running from them faster, but in opening your eyes. When the dream evaporates, everything in the dream goes with it.

The Course states:

> Miracles enable you to heal the sick and raise the dead because you made sickness and death yourself, and can therefore abolish both. *You* are a miracle, capable of creating in the likeness of your Creator. Everything else is your own nightmare, and does not exist. Only the creations of light are real.

> — T-1.I.24:1-3

The Course is telling us that no illness can hurt you, no matter how serious the world believes it is. Cancer is no more of a threat to your well-being than a cut on your hand. Both conditions are the stuff of dreams, and as such neither has more substance than the other. From a worldly point of view, this is preposterous. According to accepted belief, cancer is life-threatening and a small cut is not. From the viewpoint of miracle-mindedness, however, you are not in trouble in either case. "I am in danger nowhere in the world" (W, Lesson 244). Because your true nature is spiritual, you cannot be touched, affected, changed, damaged, or killed by any earthly condition or situation.

You are not changed by what is changeable (W-277.1:4). The body comes and goes. Your spirit is forever. Your true self is not subject to disease or any of the "slings and arrows of outrageous fortune." Anything contrary to life and love are figments of a limitation fantasy. Only the creations of light are real.

## Who Must Wake Up First?

Ramana Maharshi said, "A dreamer dreams that all the characters in his dream must wake up before he can wake up." This brilliant description of the illusion of separation unveils by contrast the express route to enlightenment.

The ego cites endless prerequisites for inner peace. There is always some change that must take place in the outer world, especially in the behavior of other people, before you can relax, feel safe, or be happy. Your husband must quit drinking, your wife should curb her shopping, the kids need to get better grades, the guy next door better quit yelling at his kids while you're trying to sleep, losing ten pounds would render you sufficiently attractive to meet your soul mate. And when will those people in the Middle East ever quit fighting?

Peace is always just on the other side of the next thing that has to change. The ego's list of preconditions for healing is long enough to ensure that the goal will never be reached. As soon as some of the conditions are fulfilled, new unmet prerequisites take their place. In this way, happiness is permanently delayed and malcontent perpetuated. The fact that lots of people agree with you, all founding their well-being on outer change, seals emptiness's victory over contentment.

But if all the characters in your world are simply actors populating your dream, you don't need for them or any other conditions to change before you can wake up. Your freedom depends on your change of mind.

ACIM tells us that the only place to seek healing is *within* and the only time to do it is *now.* "Heaven is here. There is nowhere else. Heaven is now. There is no other time" (M-24.6:4–7). The Course cuts through every illusion we have been taught about all the actions we must accomplish, or that others must do to please us, before we can be happy. "Enlightenment is but a recognition, not a change at all" (W-188.1:4). The only thing we are ever required to change is our perception. "Heaven is the decision I must make" (W, Lesson 138).

The goal of *A Course in Miracles* is not behavior management. It is consciousness upgrade. The ego finds it more appealing to try to change the world than to change your mind, because you will never change enough things in the world to make you happy, and you will always perceive gaps and grievances. To change your mind is to undo gaps and grievances at their source, and thus unplug the illusions that make the world seem so solid and formidable.

> What difference does the content of a dream make in reality? One either sleeps or wakens. There is nothing in between.
>
> — W-140.2:5-7

## When You Awake, You Will Remember Everything

The rock group The Band sang a song entitled "When You Awake," in which the chorus states that when you awake you will remember everything. I wonder if they realized that they were capturing the essence of *A Course in Miracles*. We have all been asleep and we are all awakening.

Ultimately there is only one miracle: the shift in awareness from the tyranny of fear to the healing presence of love. Miracles *seem* like many because there appear to be many different situations that need a miracle. But the one and only miracle is that everything unlike love does not exist and only love is real. All other miracles are in the service of this one.

> You have chosen a sleep in which you have had bad dreams, but the sleep is not real and God calls you to awake. There will be nothing left of your dream when you hear Him, because you will awaken . . . When you wake you will see the truth around you and in you, and you will no longer believe in dreams because they will have no reality for you. Yet the Kingdom and all that you have created there will have great reality for you, because they are beautiful and true.
>
> — T-6.IV.6:3-4,7-8

# 18

# THE HAPPY DREAM

In the Book of Genesis we are told that "a deep sleep fell upon Adam" (Genesis 2:21), but nowhere does the Bible say that he woke up (T-2.I.3:6). We are all Adam still asleep, dreaming we are separate from God and each other. *A Course in Miracles* seeks to awaken us from our slumber, not by throwing cold water on us while we sleep, but by meeting us within the dream and guiding us to the doorstep of reality. The Course works smartly, gently, and steadily to dislodge us from the illusions that bind us, by way of small, firm, consistent steps from emotional conundrum to freedom.

ACIM calls the bridge to awakening "the happy dream." In the happy dream, we walk the world awhile longer, still driving the kids to soccer practice, downloading smartphone apps, standing in line at the bank, and spending our days in ways familiar to the world. Yet the dream is no longer a nightmare. It is one of inner reward, meaning, and purpose. The peace of God becomes the foundation of our life rather than anxiety and conflict. The events, experiences, and relationships of the world become stepping-stones to heaven. The world is transformed from a prison ruled by terror to a temple consecrated by love.

> The Holy Spirit, ever practical in His wisdom, accepts your dreams and uses them as means for waking. You would have used them to remain asleep. I said before that the first change, before dreams disappear, is that your dreams of fear are changed to happy dreams.
>
> — T-18.II.6:1-3

## The Answer to Illusions

The ego does not want you to wake up because it fears that the kingdom it has fabricated would dissolve. And it is correct. So it does what it always does when confronted with peace: it reverts to fear and intensifies the illusions that keep the nightmare in force. The Holy Spirit, recognizing that a part of our mind wages war against healing, comforts us thus:

> Fear not that you will be abruptly lifted up and hurled into reality. Time is kind, and if you use it on behalf of reality, it will keep gentle pace with you in your transition. The urgency is only in dislodging your mind from its fixed position here. This will not leave you homeless and without a frame of reference.
>
> — T-16.VI.8:1-4

In the happy dream, we retain a sense of individuality in which we live in a body, experience contrast, and interact with people apparently separate from us. Yet because we have chosen love as our guide rather than fear, our experience of the dream is one of joy, not sorrow. The sun still rises and sets, but our days are founded in timelessness. Our relationships yield soul reward rather than serving as breeding grounds for attack and despair. Our body becomes a venue through which we extend kindness, rather than an object to be worshipped for its own sake. The ego still exists, but it serves us rather than bullies us, for its purpose is to uplift the world rather than harp on judgment, error, and sin. The movie we watch on the screen of appearances changes from a horror movie to a love story.

Upon discovering the happy dream, your purpose is no longer to escape the world, but to use the world on behalf of healing. Life becomes your friend. The world is new because you are new. As Marcel Proust declared, the real voyage of discovery consists not in seeking new landscapes, but in having new eyes.

## *Illusion and Compassion*

While I was presenting a seminar in Japan, a student posed this question: "I asked an ACIM teacher, 'How are we to relate to the devastating disaster of 2011 in which a huge earthquake and tsunami killed many people and wrought massive destruction in our country?' The teacher replied, 'It was all an illusion. It didn't really happen.' But I did not find that answer very satisfying. What would you say about that disaster and ones like it?"

I told the student that the answer was technically correct but not immediately helpful. It represents a kind of "ACIM fundamentalism," which quotes the letter of the law but misses the spirit behind the teaching. The purpose of *A Course in Miracles* is to bring humanity release from pain. It defines healing as relief from fear. The Course states many times that its teachings must be practical. To tell someone whose entire family has just died in a tsunami, and whose home and business have been destroyed in an earthquake, that nothing really happened does not assuage suffering. Such an answer requires too great a leap in consciousness from where the person stands to the ultimate reality beyond appearances. Instead, you must guide the distressed person to the next level of relief. He requires compassion, not philosophy.

The entire *Course in Miracles* is an act of compassion. Jesus could have sat in his golden heaven at the right hand of God and decided to leave the mass of humanity writhing in pain because "it was all an illusion" and "nothing really happened." Instead, he reached into humanity and offered a teaching that meets us where we stand and lifts us beyond our current predicament. A teacher initiates transformation by joining with the student where the student lives, rather than demanding that the student meet the teacher where the teacher lives. The ultimate goal is to lift the student to the highest level of consciousness, but that happens in gentle steps, not demanding quantum leaps of which the student is currently incapable.

I told the questioner that, in response to the disaster, I would simultaneously work from two different levels. I would keep in mind that indeed the entire event was an illusion and ultimately there is no loss or death. At the same time I would recognize that the experience felt real to those who went through it, and I would do everything I could to help relieve suffering in tangible ways. I would donate money, clothing, or medical supplies to a relief fund; or volunteer to help clean up the mess; or provide housing to refugees; or offer a listening ear, counseling, or prayer; or whatever came before me to lighten the burden of those affected. That would be more meaningful and helpful than to tell those who felt victimized that nothing had happened. For those people, something did happen, and compassion calls for service in action.

Kindness is the mark of spiritual maturity. Anyone can spout philosophy. A smaller number of teachers are willing to dive into illusion to extricate humanity from it.

## The Best Use of the News

It's easy to judge the world for its evil deeds and cruel twists. Yet we can use the events of the world as a stage to create transformation. New York philanthropist Milton Petrie scanned the newspaper every morning to see whom he could help. One day he read about a beautiful young model whose face had been severely knifed by thugs. The article showed heartrending photographs of three long hideous scars that ran the length of both cheeks and her forehead; a hundred stitches had been required to put her face back together. A Venus had become a Frankenstein.

Moved by the woman's plight, Petrie called the model to his office and told her that he would give her $20,000 a year for the rest of her life. Thrilled to receive such kindness in the wake of her anguish, she had numerous surgeries that restored her skin and face to loveliness.

Petrie also paid the living expenses of the family of a New York City policeman who had become disabled when he was shot in the line of duty. He further set up trust funds for the children of several officers who had been killed. Petrie delved into the darkest news solely for the purpose of making lives lighter. He mastered the happy dream.

I watched a documentary about cosmetic surgeons who donated their services to help people who had become disfigured, primarily women who had been beaten. In each case there was a moment when the doctor removed the bandages, and the woman looked in the mirror to see her new face for the first time. All the recipients burst into tears. A few hours of the surgeons' time led to a lifetime of feeling better for their patients. Their kindness transcended the cruelty that preceded them and facilitated the triumph of love over evil.

## *Is Chocolate on the Approved List?*

ACIM tells us, "All real pleasure comes from doing God's Will" (T-1.VII.1:4). At first this may sound like finger-shaking fundamentalism admonishing us to deny ourselves, mortify the flesh, become celibate, and retreat to a monastery. *Not so.* The Course is simply urging us to keep our priorities in order: Spirit first, all else in its service. Every experience becomes an opportunity to bring more light to the world. Then we know a kind of pleasure that goes far beyond what the world has to offer, "the peace that passes all understanding" (Philippians 4:7).

The film *Groundhog Day* maps the route from the nightmare to the happy dream. Sourpuss weatherman Phil Connors wakes up each morning to the same hellish day. Phil's first reaction to his repetitive scenario is despair. Then, to distract and placate himself, he dives into an orgy of indulgences, from scarfing down mega-caloric desserts to stealing cars to bedding hotties. This only depresses Phil further, to the point that he tries to kill himself—but even *that* doesn't work. He seems doomed to live that fateful bleak day forever.

Finally Phil experiments with the idea of helping people, doing what he can to make their lives better. He's so bored anyway, what does he have to lose? Phil catches a kid falling out of a tree, changes a flat tire for a group of elderly women, and learns to play the piano to entertain the locals. Gradually his attitude shifts from depression to joy, until one morning he wakes up from the nightmare, the woman he loves at his side. He didn't know how to love her when he was steeped in selfishness, but now that his heart has opened, he can give and receive real love. *That's* the happy dream.

So is chocolate on the approved list in the happy dream? Is there hot sex in the kingdom of heaven? Would a spiritual master shop at Nordstrom or play craps in Vegas? ACIM instructs us that the quality of life is not about *what* you do, but *why* and *how* you do it. The Course asks us to evaluate all actions we are contemplating by asking ourselves, *What is this for?* and *What do I hope to gain?* Your answers to these questions will determine whether you enter the happy dream or deepen the nightmare. If your job is simply a paycheck, you remain spiritually impoverished. If you say yes to a marriage proposal because you are afraid you will never find anyone else, you might as well pick up the divorce papers with your marriage certificate. If you have a vendetta against someone, remember the Chinese adage "When planning revenge, be sure to dig two graves."

If, on the other hand, your job is an expression of passion and purpose, universal law will bolster your success. If you marry someone because you love him *as he is* and your life is better when you are with him, that union is blessed. If you can let go of resenting your ex and move on, your next relationship will bear sweeter fruit. When joy is your motivation, joy is your result.

So is chocolate on the approved list? The question is misleading. Inner peace is on the approved list, and fear and guilt are not. The guilty mind can turn any act into a reason for condemnation. The innocent mind interprets all acts in favor of love. Love yourself no matter what you do, and what is not of love will be replaced by what is truly valuable.

## Wood and Water

A Zen maxim tells us, "Before enlightenment, chop wood and carry water. After enlightenment, chop wood and carry water." Enlightened people do many things that most people do. The only difference is that they are filled from within rather than seeking from without.

> There is a way of living in the world that is not here, although it seems to be. You do not change appearance, though you smile more frequently. Your forehead is serene; your eyes are quiet. And the ones who walk the world as you do recognize their own. Yet those who have not yet perceived the way will recognize you also, and believe that you are like them, as you were before.
>
> — W-155.1:1-5

Some of the most enlightened souls on the planet are simple, humble, unassuming people you would never think of as spiritual masters. They are waitresses, bus drivers, and appliance repairmen who have chosen kindness as their purpose. They may never have heard of *A Course in Miracles* or any formal spiritual path, but their paths are miraculous because they are merciful. As Jewish theologian Abraham Joshua Heschel noted, "When I was young, I admired clever people. Now that I am old, I admire kind people."

You will be in the world for yet a while. You will have to decide what to have for dinner, choose who to be married to (or not), and figure out the latest version of Windows. *A Course in Miracles* simply asks you to hold all of these activities lightly and remember that the only real choice is between gladness and sorrow. Happiness has nothing to do with the forms the world takes, and everything to do with the vision you are using to see the world. Meeting God is not reserved for the moment your spirit leaves your body. It is reserved for the moment you choose it. In the happy dream, what you seek is already where you are.

Love has not been hiding from us. We have been hiding from love. When the nightmare shifts to a happy dream, we are very close to home.

# Why Is the Course So Long?

Complicated minds create complicated issues, ask complicated questions, and require complicated answers. The purpose of *A Course in Miracles* is to heal complicated minds by guiding our thoughts from the labyrinth of complexity to the salvation of simplicity.

The real *Course in Miracles* is just 14 words long:

> Nothing real can be threatened.
> Nothing unreal exists.
> Herein lies the peace of God.

> — T-In.2:2-4

All the words that follow are commentary, illuminating this one truth from a thousand different vantage points.

The author of the Course recognized that few people would take such a simple truth and apply it to their lives until they found liberation. The intellect requires clarification, repetition, explanation, rational understanding, and continuous practical applications. So Jesus said, in effect, "Here are another 497,226 words and 1,187 more pages for you to chew on. Then you will feel that you've gotten something of value."

You could complete your study of *A Course in Miracles* after these 14 words.

But then you would have to live them. The remainder of the Course is given to help you do just that.

# 19

# HOW TO BE A MIRACLE WORKER

*A Course in Miracles* tells us that not only are we entitled to miracles (W, Lesson 77), but we are entitled to be miracle workers. To the ego this seems arrogant, but to *not* claim your power to work miracles is *more* arrogant. When you deny your ability to heal, you are rejecting your identity as a vessel through which the Holy Spirit can and will change lives (W, Lessons 152, 154).

Being a miracle worker does not require a secret mantra, exotic potions, throaty chants, shamanic initiation, showbiz antics, or an audience of thousands. It simply asks you to deliver your unique gifts as you walk through everyday life. Thus the world is transformed from a dreary task to a platform for awakening.

While passing through the Honolulu airport, I stopped to look at some items in a shop window. A security guard approached me and struck up a casual conversation. She asked me where I was headed, and I told her I was on my way to Japan to teach some classes. "What do you teach?" she asked.

"I help people get in touch with their passion and purpose and live authentically," I told her.

She perked up. "Then give me some tips, would you?"

I asked her what was going on in her life.

"I'm the single mother of nine children," she told me. "Most of my time goes to my kids."

I was touched by her dedication to her family. "Is there anything you would like to do for yourself?" I asked. "What could you do to nurture your own spirit?"

Tears came to her eyes as she showed me her hand. "I'd just like to get my nails done. That would make me feel pretty."

I told her, "Then please do get your nails done. You're worth it. You give so much to your kids. You deserve what makes you happy." The woman smiled and replied, "I know you're right."

I took her address and later sent her a few of my books. That encounter was one of the highlights of my journey, the kind of moment that makes any day worthwhile.

## The Ripple Effect

ACIM tells us, "A miracle is never lost. It may touch many people you have not even met, and produce undreamed of changes in situations of which you are not even aware" (T-1.I.45:1–2). Because our vision of life is usually nearsighted, we don't always see the effects of our actions that spring from love. Yet the good you do reaches far more of the universe than you realize. Never be discouraged if you have offered a kindness that does not seem to be received. On some level it *is* received, and it will be passed along to others. American historian Henry Brooks Adams noted, "A teacher affects eternity; he can never tell where his influence stops."

One of my early books, *Joy Is My Compass,* did not sell as well as my other books, and eventually it went out of print. I wondered if perhaps the book was not well written or it did not offer value to readers. I began to wonder if it had been worth the time and work to write it.

Then at a seminar a woman shared this story:

I had a vision to open up an AIDS hospice, but I doubted myself and hesitated. Then I read your book *Joy Is My Compass.* Your ideas and stories gave me the inspiration and courage to carry out my plan. Now I am so glad I did! I have taken in many men afflicted with AIDS and helped them die with dignity. These good souls were spurned and rejected by their friends and families, and had no one to support them. I gave them love and acceptance, and helped them pass on with grace. This work has been a huge blessing to me and the patients. I couldn't have done it without the inspiration I received from your book.

Upon hearing those words, I felt extremely glad I had written that book. It didn't matter if it did not become a bestseller. If nothing else happened as a result of that book besides the AIDS hospice project that woman initiated, it was totally worth writing it. It is the honor of a lifetime to contribute to those men departing this world in the presence of love.

## Time Capsule Miracles

When you claim a miracle for yourself, you claim it for everyone you touch. Remember, "When I am healed, I am not healed alone" (W, Lesson 137). In the world of appearances, it may take time for a miracle to manifest. But time is an illusion, as is the *apparent* gap between giving and receiving. Because everything is happening at once, giving and receiving occur simultaneously. It's only in the realm of separation that they *seem* to be divided.

When I was a teenager, I adopted Orthodox Judaism as my religion. For seven years I practiced the strict rituals. Eventually I tired of the dogma. One year during a holiday that requires Jews to fast, I began to question the rule. I was hungry and I didn't understand why I was not eating. The only reason I was fasting was because I was afraid God would punish me if I didn't. In that moment I realized that fear was not a good enough reason to do a religious act, and it is certainly not a healthy foundation on which to live a life. So I ate a piece of cake, which signaled the end of my participation in the Orthodox religion.

That defining moment catapulted me from my religious path onto my spiritual path. I began a passionate, intensive study that took me around the world, connected me with extraordinary teachers, opened doors to fascinating new worlds, and completely changed my life. My quest culminated in my writing books and teaching seminars received by many thousands of people over many years.

More than 30 years after that turning point, I recounted the story at a residential seminar. Afterward a participant named Ray approached me and shook my hand firmly. "Thank you for eating that cake," he told me.

Ray's feedback was a shorthand way of saying, "You eating that cake set into motion a series of events that led to us being together for a deeply rewarding experience. Thank you for following your heart's true path, which is now entwined with mine."

Any act of kindness you do for yourself or others on Earth bears heavenly fruit. You taste such fruit twice: once in the moment you act from love, and again when you see its effects. Sometimes you see the effect immediately, sometimes later, and sometimes not at all. "Miracles . . . may not always have observable effects" (T-1.I.35). Yet very often you will receive a synchronistic or miraculous confirmation that your act of sincere intention has made someone else's life better. There is no greater reward than this.

## Temporarily More and Less

We take turns performing miracles for one another. In the world, we experience a *seeming* alteration of supply and lack. Sometimes you are more aware of supply than other people are, and sometimes others are more in touch with supply than you are. When you experience a sense of abundance, you are in a position to perform miracles for others, because in that moment you are in alignment with universal truth. When others are more connected to abundance than you, they can perform miracles for you. "Miracles are healing because they supply a lack; they are performed by those who temporarily have more for those who temporarily have less" (T-1.I:8).

At one time I needed some publicity photos taken. My friend Monique, a talented professional photographer, came to my house and spent an afternoon shooting photos, some of which turned out to be excellent and quite useful. I asked Monique what I owed her in exchange for the photos, and she told me not to worry about it; maybe I could help her out sometime. I felt indebted to her, and several times thought about sending her a check. When I did, an inner voice told me to just relax; things would work out. Several years later I presented a Hawaii retreat on the theme of abundance. Monique told me she would like to attend, but at the time she was not in a position to pay the tuition. I was happy to return her favor, so I gave her the program tuition free. What goes around comes around.

It is as important to receive miracles as it is to give them. When you allow someone to help you, you afford that person the joy of being a miracle worker. Many people, especially those who grew up in a religion that taught guilt, have a hard time receiving. They believe it is saintly or responsibly sacrificial to deny themselves; giving is virtuous, but receiving is selfish. This is another example of upside-down thinking. When you allow someone to sincerely help you, you help them. They receive the reward of giving, while you receive the joy of receiving. Miracle working is a win-win experience. Let's remember, "[Miracles] bring more love both to the giver *and* the receiver" (T-1.I.9:3).

## Credit Where Credit Is Due

Your ego, or personality, is not the source of miracles. God is. "It is not I, but the Father within me that does the work," said Jesus (John 14:10). The love that animates the entire universe brings all good to the world. You are the vital avenue through which this holy transmission occurs. To keep roles in order, always give credit to God as the source of all blessings. Never identify yourself as the source of miracles. If you do, you are setting yourself up for a tragic fall. Bloated egos always get shredded. Humility will help you avoid such pitfalls.

I met a radiant Muslim healer named Ishvara. When her clients thanked her for their healing, she would always say, "All praise is due to Allah." Although I met Ishvara many years ago, that phrase still rings in my mind. It was a graceful way to take the spotlight off the personality and return it to Higher Power, where it belongs. You do not diminish yourself by offering credit to God. You glorify the divinity within you. "Be humble before Him, and yet great *in* Him" (T-15.IV.3:1).

If you feel tired, fatigued, or burned-out after offering your service, you have forgotten that Higher Power is the real miracle worker. I heard a student ask a famous healer, "Why do I feel so fried after I do several healing sessions?" The healer deftly replied, "Because you think you are the healer."

I know healers who have infinite energy and never get tired. They do superhuman acts and achieve results that bless thousands. They understand that Source Energy, not the personality, is achieving the results. Jesus promised, "Even greater things than I, shall he do" (John 14:12). That would be *you*. Jesus was affirming that the capacity to perform miracles belongs to *all of us*. In partnership with Great Spirit, you will succeed.

> My eyes, my tongue, my hands, my feet today
> Have but one purpose; to be given Christ
> To use to bless the world with miracles.
>
> — W, Lesson 353

## The Ultimate Miracle

What appears to be a miraculous healing or manifestation is just the tip of the iceberg of the source of all miracles, which is love. "Miracles occur naturally as expressions of love. The real miracle is the love that inspires them. In this sense everything that comes from love is a miracle" (T-1.I.3:1–3).

You don't have to know how to perform miracles. You just have to be fully present, keep your mind and heart open, seek to help where you can, remember wholeness more than appearances of brokenness, and love more than fear. When you maintain inner peace in the face of illusions to the contrary, miracles follow. Then you watch them in awe, along with the recipients.

Don't get hung up on the manifestation aspect of miracles. "Miracles as such do not matter" (T-1.I.2:1). Never try to perform a miracle. Trying means that the ego has gotten into the act. Egos try. Spirit *does.* As miracle worker Yoda said, "Try not. Do or do not. There is no try." The experience of anxiety means you believe you are the doer. "The presence of fear is a sure sign that you are trusting in your own strength" (W-48.3:1).

ACIM tells us, "Consciously selected miracles can be misguided" (T-1.I.5:3). Set a goal if you like, but leave the details to the Holy Spirit, who has access to far broader resources than you do. Be open to receive the goal you have requested, and at the same time leave space for something even better to happen. Higher Power has a bottomless bag of tricks that will astound you. Sometimes Spirit will work miracles through you, and sometimes through other people or other avenues. It doesn't matter how healing happens. It just matters that it happens.

You will be guided as to the miracles you are to perform. Don't stress about where or how you can most help. The divine dispatcher will give you your assignment and the means to carry it out. You are working for a very big company.

> Thus will each gift to Him be multiplied a thousandfold and tens of thousands more. And when it is returned to you, it will surpass in might the little gift you gave as much as does the radiance of the sun outshine the tiny gleam a firefly makes an uncertain moment and goes out. The steady brilliance of this light remains and leads you out of darkness, nor will you be able to forget the way again.
>
> — W-97.6:1-3

# 20

# TEACH
# ONLY LOVE

The world is confused about how teaching occurs. You have been taught that teaching is accomplished through words in a classroom. The teacher spouts an idea, the students record it on paper or computer, they memorize it for the final exam, and if they repeat it well, they are assumed to have learned. Real teaching, *A Course in Miracles* tells us, occurs by the energy you broadcast through the quality of your being. At every moment you are teaching love or you are teaching fear. *There are no other lessons.*

If you consider the teachers who have affected your life most profoundly, it was not the information they gave you that transformed you. It was how they treated you and how you felt in their presence. One of my greatest teachers was a young rabbi named Stuie. I met him when I was 14 years old, pimply faced, braces on my teeth, hormones raging with no healthy avenue of expression. I was living in the worst part of town with many seedy influences. My world was dense and bewildering.

One day I felt oddly guided to attend a youth brunch at my synagogue, where Stuie gave an impassioned speech. He was the first person I had met who had a real relationship with God. He exuded inspiration and passion, and I was moved by his magnetic presence. I joined the synagogue youth group and Stuie become my mentor. I spent most of my free time with him and other teenagers in that positive atmosphere. Rabbi Stuie's influence on my life was immeasurable. He encouraged me to run for president of the youth group, and soon I was giving speeches to the kids and the synagogue. My mentor saw the best in me, and his vision brought my talents forth. That rabbi changed the entire direction of my life, for which I am forever grateful. He was a true teacher of God.

You, too, are a teacher of God in the way you carry yourself and the quality of your being. One day I was hurrying through the San Francisco airport amidst hordes of travelers hustling to and from airplanes. Then I noticed a man walking toward me who had an aura of peace about him. He was not wearing the robe of a priest or doing anything unusual. He was quite ordinary in his appearance. Yet his demeanor was so calm in the midst of the chaos about him that the moment I looked at him I felt relaxed and peaceful. He was a mobile blessing unit. I saw this fellow for but a few seconds, we had no conversation, and I have never seen him again. I do not know his name or any information about his life. Although that brief interaction occurred many years ago, I still remember him, and I refer to him in my books and lectures. Such is the transformational power a human being can generate simply by being at peace.

> A teacher of God is anyone who chooses to be one. His qualifications consist solely in this; somehow, somewhere he has made a deliberate choice in which he did not see his interests as apart from someone else's.
>
> — M-1.1:1-2

## Your Only Mission

Many people set out on missions to convert others to their religion or group. Well-meaning as such people may be, they often do not recognize their deeper mission. "When you have accepted your mission to extend peace you will find peace . . ." (T-12.VII.11:1).

You are not here to convert others. You are here to convert your own consciousness. When you are connected to your Source, you call others to live their potential. The goal to change others is a distraction from your true goal of changing your own mind. It's easier to talk other people into coming to church than it is to face and conquer your own fears, inner demons, judgments, and sense of emptiness. If you need others to follow your dogma in order for you to feel adequate, you are proceeding from a sense of lack, which never begets healthy results.

As you find your wholeness and live from it, the world will be transformed by your model and you will leave a trail of healing in your wake.

## A Whole New Purpose

ACIM states that you will be appalled when you realize what you are truly here for (T-17.V.5:6). You thought you were here to get stuff, prove yourself, and find people to love you. Instead you are here get peace, be yourself, and find people to love. You thought you were here to fix the world. Instead you are here to appreciate what is before you and see the world through new eyes. You thought you were here to teach, while you are here to learn. Ultimately teaching and learning are one (M-In.1:5). You cannot teach without learning and you cannot learn without teaching. When you teach only love, you learn only love. Then you graduate from the school of illusion and accept the diploma of inner peace, the real degree we are all here to attain.

You have had many teachers in your life, and you have taught many. You will teach more. As a student of *A Course in Miracles,* you forever upgrade your notion of teaching and learning. Your purpose is far more profound than you have been taught, and the route to your destiny far simpler. You are here to transform the world by changing your thoughts about the world and who you are in it. You are a loving being living in a universe founded in love. Remember but this, and you will master the only lesson you are here to learn. Then you will teach it constantly without even trying.

Teach only love, for that is what you are.

— T-6.I.13:2

## Do I Need to Attend a *Course in Miracles* Study Group?

*A Course in Miracles* is a self-study system to deepen your relationship with yourself and your Higher Power. There is nothing in the Course that requires you to attend a class or study with a group. Practiced diligently, ACIM can and will take you all the way home. Your teacher is the Holy Spirit, your classroom is life, and your fellow students are everyone you encounter.

If you feel that participating in a class or group will help you, it can. There is value in being in the presence of others committed to living consciously. In the Buddhist and Hindu spiritual traditions, adherents are urged to participate in *satsang,* the company of truth.

If you attend an ACIM study group, you may meet people who have been studying the Course longer than you have, and thus you can deepen your understanding by hearing their perspectives and experience. Even more important, if the people in the group are living the principles of the Course and healing their minds, lives, and others, you will benefit immensely from their example.

If you attend an ACIM study group, choose one that is heart and experience centered rather than intellectual only. Some study groups become entrenched in erudite discussions to the point that the conversation becomes an exercise in intellectual gymnastics rather than soul awakening. Stay true to the spirit of the Course rather than becoming distracted by the letter of the law. *A Course in Miracles* is a love letter from God. Academically dissecting a love letter is antithetical to the poetry it exudes. Savoring it brings the deepest reward.

I have a great deal of experience with group study of the Course, since many years ago I cofounded a *Course in Miracles* living community. Twenty-seven ACIM students got together and rented a vacant convent building, complete with dormitory rooms, a chapel, a large meeting hall, and an industrial kitchen. We committed to live together and study the Course for one year. The group included three single mothers with children, several gay men, a high school teacher, one woman's elderly mother, and a number of business professionals. The group was colorfully diverse.

We named our community "Miracle Manor." Each morning we met in the chapel and studied the Lesson for the day, then went off to our jobs, families, and daily errands. We gathered again in the evening to review the Lesson, read from the Text, meditate, and pray. During that year, many luminary teachers, healers, and musicians passed through those hallowed halls, offering a smorgasbord of stimulating classes, lectures, and concerts.

I could write an entire book about Miracle Manor, but here I will simply say that we all had plenty of chances to practice forgiveness. Initially egos roared in the midst of newness, uncertainty, life changes, and sharing intimate living space with a group of strangers. Everyone went crazy. I remember coming to breakfast one morning to find a woman crying into her scrambled eggs. One fellow bedded three of the women in the group during the first month and then moved out because he "had to take care of [his] sick grandmother." One woman locked herself in her room at the end of week one and we never saw her again. The miracle house turned into a nuthouse!

Yet as the year went on, there was transformation. Because the participants were sincere in practicing the Course, the insanity gradually shifted to caring, kindness, and mutual support. Selfish interests gave way to joining. After six months the group gelled, and love became the predominant theme. By the time the year's journey was complete, we beheld the light within each other and found immense value in our shared adventure. Yet we did go through hell to get to heaven. Not because we had to. Because we allowed ego to run the show for a while.

So do you need to attend a group to study *A Course in Miracles*? It doesn't really matter. You take your consciousness with you wherever you go. If you study alone, you will meet yourself. If you study with a group, you will meet yourself. Every moment is an opportunity to remember what's important, and to the extent you do, you will be healed.

# 21

# HOW THE WORLD WILL END

Every few years a preacher announces that the world will come to an end on a certain upcoming date. Or astrologers pronounce the end of a cosmic cycle. Or the Mayan calendar will run out. Or an asteroid will collide with Earth. Then a favored few will ascend to heaven while the rest of humanity remains consigned to a fiery pit. After one recent end-days announcement, some clever people offered *tribulation pet-care insurance*: If you ascend while your pet stays behind on Earth, a thoughtful sitter will watch your pooch or pussycat for only $50 (nonrefundable). (Personally, I wouldn't trust any heaven that would not take my dog.) Then the predicted judgment day comes and goes without mishap. The preacher says he miscalculated; the *real* tribulation date is a few more years down the road. And the beat goes on.

The end of the world, *A Course in Miracles* explains, is not an event in time. It is a *shift in perception*. When we transfer our attention from the world of sin, separation, and suffering, to the realm of innocence, well-being, and grace, we have transcended the realm of illusion and come home to reality. The end of the world will come when you have no more use for it. So you don't have to worry about the world ending. It will stay as long as you want it to. The hitch, ACIM explains, is that you want the unreal world more than the real world. The problem, then, is not that the world might end. The problem is that the world might *not* end. Nothing could be more rapturous than the end of life as we know it. Not because life is bad. Because life as we have come to know it is a bizarre distortion of life as we were meant to live it.

The Manual for Teachers poignantly explains it thus:

The world will end in joy, because it is a place of sorrow. When joy has come, the purpose of the world has gone. The world will end in peace, because it is a place of war. When peace has come, what is the purpose of the world? The world will end in laughter, because it is a place of tears. Where there is laughter, who can longer weep?

— M-14.5:1-6

What we regard as the world has been cleverly designed by the ego to hide the real world. Fear masks love, smallness eclipses magnitude, and time strangles eternity. In every way it is the opposite of the world God created. The end of the world as we know it is a blessed event, for when we withdraw our investment in hell, all that is left is heaven.

## One Name or Many?

The world will end when the awareness of the omnipresence of God replaces the belief in bodies severed from each other and love. Science-fiction master Arthur C. Clarke penned a brilliant short story called "The Nine Billion Names of God," in which two computer programmers are hired by a group of monks in a Tibetan lamasery. The monks believe that when all the names of God have been discovered, the purpose of this world will be complete and the physical dimension will disappear. In an effort to capture all those names—nine billion, to be exact—the monks import the American programmers to code their computer to spit out all the combinations and permutations of the letters in their alphabet, generating all the names of God at lightning speed, thus hastening the end of the world of suffering.

The programmers, skeptical but happy to be paid for the job, play along with the monks and create the program as requested. But the geeks fear that when the computer finishes the job and the world is still very much here, they will be blamed. So they delay the final printout until after they have departed the lamasery. At the crucial moment the programmers sit on ponies at a distance from the lamasery, speculating about the disappointment the monks must be feeling. Just then they look up and notice that "without any fuss, the stars were going out."

This clever tale bears powerful metaphysical symbolism. When we finally replace all separate names with the One Name, manifest creation will have fulfilled its purpose and we will dwell in our true essence. The end of the illusory world of discrete, disconnected forms will yield to the experience of the real world as the unified being of God. "Hear O Israel, the Lord our God, the Lord is One" (Deuteronomy 6:4).

## Where Is the World?

*A Course in Miracles* tells us that the world "out there" is nothing more than the out-picturing of the thoughts we hold about it. The Course goes as far as to say, "There is no world! This is the central thought the course attempts to teach" (W-132.6:2–3).

Later in the Workbook we read:

From insane wishes comes an insane world. From judgment comes a world condemned. And from forgiving thoughts a gentle world comes forth, with mercy for the holy Son of God . . .

— W-325.1:4-6

So the end of the world as you know it is exactly that: the end of the world you know. Yet because the world you know is so very different from the world God knows, the end of the world is nothing more than the end of the tiny stream of thought that has defined the constricted world you see. It is the advent of a river of life far wider, deeper, and richer than the little self can fathom. The end of the world comes when you change your mind about it. It's not a big dramatic Hollywood cataclysm replete with thousands of extras retching and screaming. It is as gentle and relief giving as opening the windows and curtains of a long-closed stuffy room and receiving light and air that brings life where there was none.

## Finally, a World That Makes Sense

We define the world by finite measurements. It is prescribed by the square footage of your house, the cost of your new car, the size of the diamond on your engagement ring, the number of your Twitter followers, stock market trends, and the length of the scar your cousin proudly displays as a medal from his operation. None of these quantities have anything to do with the real world. People are in pain because we have invested our attention in a meaningless world. The world of separation ends when you become more interested in the infinite than the finite.

> The world will end in an illusion, as it began. Yet will its ending be an illusion of mercy. The illusion of forgiveness, complete, excluding no one, limitless in gentleness, will cover it, hiding all evil, concealing all sin and ending guilt forever. So ends the world that guilt had made, for now it has no purpose and is gone.
>
> — M-14.1:2-5

Pray for the end of the world. Pray for the end of fear, loss, suffering, and death. The world as we know it makes no sense. End a senseless world by coming to your senses. Become so immersed in truth that all that is false fades from sight. Vision is a choice. We see what we want to see. Change what you want to see, and what you see will change.

## The Beginning Is at Hand

We have all seen people walking the streets of cities wearing sandwich boards proclaiming: THE END IS AT HAND. In a way, they are right. The world of sorrow must end. "The world I see holds nothing that I want" (W, Lesson 128). But that's only half the story. If sidewalk prophets told the whole story, the signs on their backs would read: AND SO IS THE BEGINNING. "Beyond this world there is a world I want" (W, Lesson 129).

End the world today by refusing to contribute to the pool of fear that has kept the world of sorrow in force. End starvation by feeding your soul. End war by ceasing the war against yourself. It is your happiness, not your pain, that will save the world. Misery has enough company.

Armageddon will not end the world. Armageddon has been going on for thousands of years, and it has not led to peace. Only healing will end the world. God has chosen you to save the world, imploring you to replace doom with the expectation of immense blessing. Then, one by one the stars in the heavens will go out, and they will be replaced with the light that you are.

> You and your brother are coming home together, after a long and meaningless journey that you undertook apart, and that led nowhere. You have found your brother, and you will light each other's way. And from this light will the Great Rays extend back into darkness and forward unto God, to shine away the past and so make room for His eternal Presence, in which everything is radiant in the light.
>
> — T-18.III.8:5-7

# 22

# GRADUATION DAY

The story is told about a yogi who left his guru to retreat in the forest and develop supernatural powers. For many years he devoted himself to learning how to walk on water. Finally he mastered the technique. Then one day his guru happened to be passing by. The yogi, eager to demonstrate his power, walked across a river while the guru watched.

"How long did it take you to learn to walk on water?" asked the guru.

"Twenty-seven years," the disciple proudly answered.

"Idiot!" the guru replied. "For fifty cents you could have taken the ferry!"

At some point each of us must question what we are seeking to accomplish during our time on Earth, and why. Some of our goals lead us to peace, and many don't. *A Course in Miracles* calls us to devote our time and our life to what is of true value. Setting out on the ACIM journey is no small undertaking. It requires diligence, commitment, sincerity, intention, and practice. As you move through the program you may wonder, "When will I finish the Course? How will I know when I'm done? When is graduation day?"

The Course tells us, "The training period is one year" (W-In.2:4). I usually laugh when I read this. I don't know anyone who has gone through the Course in a year, closed the book, and said, "There, I've got it . . . What's next?"

When I met Judith Skutch (Whitson), founder of the Foundation for Inner Peace, publisher of *A Course in Miracles,* she told me, "I will be doing the Course every day for the rest of my life." At the time I didn't understand her vision, but now I do. When you are hooked on peace, there is no returning to war. When healing is more attractive than pain, you do only what heals. When you want freedom more than bondage, you take any and all steps necessary to get and stay free.

I met a woman who did not miss one ACIM Lesson or exercise during the Workbook year. She even did all the five-minute-per-hour practice sessions prescribed in Lessons 93–110. Her entire life changed. Her health improved, along with her relationships. She became a shiny new person, a living miracle. The next time I saw her, she was going through the Course again.

I have been studying *A Course in Miracles* for 35 years. I have gone through the Workbook many times. Daily I use Course principles to make sense of my experiences; phrases from all three volumes flash into my mind hourly. Yet sometimes, such as when I get impatient with a slow driver, I am appalled by what a sluggish learner I have been. My ego has loomed large and I have found the cleverest ways to keep peace at arm's length. Sometimes I wonder if I will ever master the program. At other times, such as when I let go of a potential upset that would have previously disturbed me, I am amazed by how much I have absorbed. Yet in spite of doubts and setbacks, each time I move through the Course, my *Aha*'s increase and I recognize the stunning magnitude of the teachings. As I read the Text, I can swear that the words are new each time I open a page I have visited many times before. Each morning it seems like the day's Lesson was written the night before just for me. I think, "This is the best Lesson in the Course. I will do this Lesson for the rest of my life and be liberated!" The process of studying ACIM is in itself a miracle.

I imagine you could complete ACIM in a year if you were really intent. But then you probably wouldn't stay around very long to report on your experience. You would likely ascend and merge back into the infinite. Or perhaps you would be a bodhisattva and stick around to uplift humanity.

I asked Judith Whitson if she knew anyone who had mastered *A Course in Miracles*. She told me that Bill Thetford, co-scribe of the Course, was such a person. "Bill had forgiven everyone and everything, and he was completely at peace," she told me. That testimonial gave me confidence that there is hope for me and all of us to do the same.

Meanwhile, our Lessons on Earth call to us. We have no shortage of opportunities to practice forgiveness. Inner peace is the only benchmark of progress in the Course. Absence of peace is a call to keep practicing.

My cousin told me, "I bought an abdominal fat reducer I saw on an infomercial . . . but I sent the damn thing back—it didn't work."

"How much did you use it?"

"Oh, maybe five minutes a week."

While the Course's potential is infinite, the results you experience depend on your application. As folks in 12-step programs say, "It works if you work it." ACIM echoes, "Only what *you* have not given can be lacking in any situation" (T-17.VII.4:1). *A Course in Miracles* is far more than the three volumes or the exercises in the Workbook. It is a way of thinking and living, an attitudinal shift that affects everything you see and do. It is a global psycho-spiritual makeover.

## The Road to Here

"When will I finish the Course?" is a trick question presented by the ego. The ego is preoccupied with the future as an escape from the present, while the answer to all questions rests in the holy instant. "My present happiness is all I see" (W, Lesson 290). Each wondrous here and now will lead to the next one, and you will arrive at the end of time by rising beyond it.

In a sense, you have already finished *A Course in Miracles.* Your spirit is whole, God has already given you everything you need, and He has done everything that needs to be done (W-337.1:5). You are an eternal being, forgiven for the sins you never committed. You cannot and will not die. The hell you fear was but a scare tactic. The path you believe you still must tread has already been walked. The obstacles you perceive are already behind you. You are on "a journey without distance to a goal that has never changed" (T-8.VI.9:7). In the world of distance, there is no end to *A Course in Miracles.* In the world of Spirit, what never began cannot end.

Your need, then, is not to finish the Course. Your need is to know that you have already finished the Course. Even while a part of you is striving, your deeper, truer Self has crossed the finish line of a race you never needed to run. The purpose of the Course is to shift your identity from the seeker to the found. When you remember who you are, there is nothing left to achieve. Heaven is not a trophy you are awarded for your struggle. It is a status you accept, a blessed state of mind in which you dwell.

Along the way to here, you experience sun and clouds, peaks and valleys, breakthroughs to clarity and mires of confusion, heady exhilaration and curtains of depression. "Doubt along the way will come and go and go to come again" (C-Ep.1:2). *Just keep going.* Don't let appearances stop you. Ask Holy Spirit to do for you what you cannot do for yourself. Your prayer will surely be answered. Your prayer is *already* answered. "You cannot fail to hear me, Father. What I ask have You already given me" (W-290.2:2–3). A part of your mind is established in truth even whille illusions persist. Claim that part, and appearances contrary to love will evaporate. Only the thoughts you think with God are true.

The end of the final sentence of the Workbook, ". . . I will never leave you comfortless" (W-Ep.6:8), is Jesus's promise that no matter where you go in the world, no matter what course you study, no matter what hells seem to engulf you, your Source has not abandoned you, and peace is given the moment you ask for it. You are never more than one thought away from healing. Mighty companions walk at your side, in this world and beyond it. We do not walk alone (W, Lesson 156).

## The End of the Quest for the Holy Grail

*A Course in Miracles* is unlike many other spiritual teachings in that its goal is total freedom. It does not stop short of complete healing. You are done with the Course when you are free of fear, you are at peace with yourself, you see everyone and everything as God, and all you experience is love. As long as you are in a body, this will be a stretch to achieve, because the very idea that you believe you are in a body denies the truth that you are a spirit. Some people, the Course tells us, have attained full liberation while in a body, but that is rare. This is not to say you cannot do this. In fact, the Course promises that you will do precisely this when the time is right. For now, enlightenment proceeds in stages. A few ripe souls wake up one morning and attain freedom forever. The greater part of humanity ascends the stairway to heaven one step at a time.

Yet each step is rewarding unto itself, and the world is not a bad place to explore when you regard it through the eyes of appreciation. "Love is the way I walk in gratitude" (W, Lesson 195). The Course would have us progress as fast as possible, but not so fast that we miss steps in the dance. We drop a few more illusions daily until our lives become more of a celebration than a drudgery. Then, ACIM tells us, God will take the final step (W-168.3:2).

At some point you may decide that your study of ACIM is complete and you might choose another avenue. Or you might merge your study of the Course with another tool. Or you could put the Course aside and return to it later. Or you may recognize that staying with the Course will take you all the way home, and you will do just that. Any worthy endeavor will introduce you to your Self. All spiritual practices are a course in miracles in different packages. ACIM tells us plainly that it is not the only path. Many routes will take you to the summit. Yet there is one realization everyone finds when they reach the peak: The Holy Grail you sought was in your pack as you ascended.

*A Course in Miracles* lives forever, as you do. When Ramana Maharshi was near death, his disciples begged him, "Master, please do not leave us." He smiled and replied, "Where could I go?" Likewise, the message of ACIM is that love is everywhere, and as a being of love, so are you. The Course is the end of endings, a gateway to the infinite. When you look about you and all you see is heaven, the Course will have done its job. It will let go of your hand and release you to be the light you have sought.

A *Course in Miracles* has found you. Now all that is left is for you to find yourself. May that noble awakening come soon and last forever. May we all know ourselves as God created us. May we all know life as we were meant to live it. May we all love purely, deeply, and totally. May humanity discover its divinity, and may we all dwell in the peace of God.

# EPILOGUE

## Everything You Always Wanted to Know about ACIM but Didn't Want to Have to Read the Whole Course to Find Out

1. Only God is real. All separation is illusion.

2. You are an extension and expression of God. Everything God is, you are. Everything God is not, you are not. God is love and only love, and so are you.

3. Every thought you think, word you speak, and action you take represents your choice between love and fear. Choose love.

4. The purpose of the body is to communicate love. All other purposes of the body are in vain. Use your body to shine Spirit into the world, and it will be happy and healthy.

5. The ego is an extremely limited idea of who you are. It is not equipped to guide you and should not be consulted to make choices that bring you peace.

6. The Holy Spirit is the part of your mind connected with truth. Consult it to make wise choices, and you will thrive.

7. Beyond the apparent world is the real world, where everything you desire and deserve exists. You can step into the real world at any moment by remembering your identity as a spiritual being.

8. There is no sin. There are only errors in consciousness. You are already forgiven. All that you believe must come of your sins will never happen.

9. The purpose of all relationships is to make you happy. Appreciate and celebrate everyone, for they are lovable, as you are.

10. People who act unkindly are calling for love. Evil has no power because it does not come from God. Love is the only power.

11. There is nothing you need to do to earn salvation. You are worthy for what you are. You are already saved. You simply need to know it.

12. The universe is brimming with abundance. You have everything you need right where you stand, and you will always have all you need.

13. Your only purpose on Earth is to make it more like heaven. Worry less and laugh more.

14. There is no death. You are an eternal being. Bodies come and go, but Spirit is forever.

# LEARN MORE

To learn more about *A Course in Miracles,* I recommend you visit the website of the publisher of the Course, the Foundation for Inner Peace: www.acim.org. While there are many excellent organizations supporting study of *A Course in Miracles,* this is the original one with the greatest variety and depth of Course-related materials, including biographies and photos of the scribes, DVDs, free access to daily Lessons, audio recordings, information about the many languages into which the Course has been translated, and electronic versions of the Course, including mobile device apps.

The Foundation for Inner Peace is a nonprofit organization dedicated to uplifting humanity through *A Course in Miracles.* The organization depends on donations and is currently immersed in translating the Course into many languages (25 to date). The Foundation also donates thousands of copies of the Course. If you would like to support more people to benefit from *A Course in Miracles,* donating to the Foundation for Inner Peace or one of the many other fine Course-related organizations would be a worthy endeavor. A portion of the proceeds from this book will be donated to the Foundation for Inner Peace and other organizations proliferating *A Course in Miracles.*

# ACKNOWLEDGMENTS

A book about miracles is a result of miracles, and I am deeply grateful to all who have supported the birth of this work.

First and foremost I honor my partner and beloved Dee for her untiring heartfelt enthusiastic support for me to create and serve. I must also give credit to my loyal and eternally lovable dogs, who keep me sane when I most need to remember what's important.

I stand ever in humble gratitude to the scribes of *A Course in Miracles*, Dr. Helen Schucman and Dr. Bill Thetford for their monumental courage and efforts to deliver the Course to the world. Judith Whitson's soul contract to publish and disseminate the Course is equally significant, along with Dr. Kenneth Wapnick's contribution and dedication to proliferate the teachings, as well as the initial and current members of the Foundation for Inner Peace.

I honor my fellow students and teachers of *A Course in Miracles*, whose eloquent expression has deepened my understanding and inner peace. While many have taught and inspired me, here I will thank those with whom I have had the most direct contact and who have contributed to this book: Jon Mundy, Tony Ponticello, Robert Holden, Tom Carpenter, Jerry Jampolsky, Diane Cirincione, Ian Patrick, Michael Stillwater, Maloah Stillwater, Charley Thweatt, Paul Ferrini, Arnold Patent, Kenneth Bok, Cliff Klein, and Alden Crull.

As always, the team at Hay House has stepped up to support and proliferate this work. Ongoing huge thanks to Louise Hay, Reid Tracy, Patty Gift, and especially my editor Alex Freemon, always a delight to co-create with. Kudos to Julie Davison and Nick Welch for their brilliant graphic and interior design. The Hay House Radio team, ably guided by Diane Ray, is a blessing to me and so many avid listeners. Many thanks as well to all the staff in all the Hay House departments.

I offer my gratitude to all students of *A Course in Miracles*, in all nations at all times, past, present, and future. You bless the world by being the light that you are.

# LEARN MORE
# WITH ALAN COHEN

If you have enjoyed and benefited from *A Course in Miracles Made Easy*, you may want to deepen your understanding and inspiration by participating in Alan Cohen's in-person seminars, online courses, life coach training, or online subscription programs.

**Quote for the Day**—An inspirational quotation e-mailed to you each day (free)

**Monthly e-Newsletter**—Uplifting articles and announcements of events (free)

**Wisdom for Today**—A stimulating life lesson e-mailed to you daily

**Online Courses**—Lessons and teleseminars on relevant topics including *A Course in Miracles,* relationships, prosperity, healing, prayer, metaphysics, and time management

**ACIM Seminars/Retreats**—Join other Course students to deepen your understanding of ACIM, apply its principles to your daily life, and enjoy the fellowship of like-minded peers

**Mastery Training**—A transformational retreat in Hawaii to align your life with your passion, power, and purpose

**Life Coach Training**—Become a certified professional life coach or enhance your career and personal life with coaching skills

For information about all of these programs and new products and events, visit: www.AlanCohen.com

# ABOUT THE AUTHOR

MoniqueFeil.com

**Alan Cohen MA** is the author of many popular inspirational books, including the bestselling *The Dragon Doesn't Live Here Anymore* and the award-winning *A Deep Breath of Life*. He is a contributing writer for the #1 *New York Times* bestselling series *Chicken Soup for the Soul,* and his monthly column, 'From the Heart' is published in magazines internationally. His work has been featured on CNN and Oprah.com and in *USA Today, The Washington Post* and the book *The Top 101 Experts Who Help Us Improve Our Lives*. His books have been translated into 24 languages.

Alan hosts the popular show *Get Real* weekly on Hay House Radio, and he has been a featured presenter in the award-winning documentary *Finding Joe*, as well as the documentaries *iGod* and *Living in Light*. Alan is the founder and director of the Foundation for Holistic Life Coaching, and he keynotes and presents seminars in the field of life mastery and vision psychology. He resides with his family in Hawaii.

**www.alancohen.com**

# Hay House Titles of Related Interest

# NOTES

# NOTES

# NOTES

# NOTES

# NOTES

# NOTES

# NOTES

# NOTES

# NOTES

# NOTES

# HAY HOUSE

*Look within*

Join the conversation about latest products,
events, exclusive offers and more.

 Hay House UK

 @HayHouseUK

 @hayhouseuk

 healyourlife.com

*We'd love to hear from you!*